HOW TO M.
YOUR OWN GREETING CARDS

Also by Rosalie Brown

BROWNIES MAKE THINGS No. 1
BROWNIES MAKE THINGS No. 2
BROWNIES MAKE THINGS No. 3
BROWNIES MAKE THINGS No. 4
HANDCRAFTS FOR ALL SEASONS No. 1
HANDCRAFTS FOR ALL SEASONS No. 2
HANDCRAFTS FOR ALL SEASONS No. 3
HANDCRAFTS FOR ALL SEASONS No. 4
IDEAS FOR PACKS
MORE IDEAS FOR PACKS
THINGS TO MAKE FROM THIN CARD No. 1
THINGS TO MAKE FROM THIN CARD No. 2
BROWNIES ARE WIDE AWAKE No. 1
BROWNIES ARE WIDE AWAKE No. 2
HOW TO MAKE MASKS AND PARTY HATS No. 1
HOW TO MAKE MASKS AND PARTY HATS No. 2
HOW TO MAKE YOUR OWN DECORATIONS
HOW TO MAKE PAPER CUTS AND SILHOUETTES
GAMES FOR TRAVELLERS

With Arthur Brown

HOW TO MAKE AND PLAY INDOOR GAMES No. 1
HOW TO MAKE AND PLAY INDOOR GAMES No. 2

HOW TO MAKE
YOUR OWN GREETING CARDS

Devised and drawn

by

ROSALIE BROWN

JADE PUBLISHERS
HASLEMERE

Jade Publishers
15 Stoatley Rise
Haslemere
Surrey GU27 1AF

First published 1984

First published in this revised edition 1990

Cover illustration by Alma Spriggs
Cover design by Samantha Edwards

Typesetting by 'Keyword', Tring, Herts

Printed and bound by Hillman Printers Ltd., Frome, Somerset

British Library Cataloguing in Publication Data
Brown, Rosalie, 1910–
How to make your own greetings cards
1. Greetings cards. Making
I. Title
745.5941

ISBN 0–903461–30–7

CONTENTS

Continued

INTRODUCTION

These Greeting Cards cover almost every special message you may wish to send to friends or relations. Most of them can be easily adapted for any occasion. Many have already been made by children. Ideas for special invitation cards are also given. In the book you will find a list of special occasions for greeting cards, and this includes invitations to parties of various kinds. There is also a list of Wedding Anniversaries to help you.

It is not always easy for some people to write the greetings or verses neatly by hand, but there is no reason why you should not use the printed ones from old cards.

It is not always easy, either, to draw or copy anything, but by using the grid method explained at the back of the book, you may find this less difficult. If you need tracing paper, you will find that kitchen greaseproof paper is a good substitute – and cheaper!

Measurements are in centimetres and millimetres, and in brackets the nearest size to them in inches.

ROSALIE BROWN

MATERIALS USED

Black ballpoint
Black ink
Blotting paper
Brass two-pronged paper clip
Brown gummed paper roll
Brown wrapping paper
Calendars of views
Cocktail stick
Coloured cartridge papers
Coloured gummed paper
Coloured magazines
Coloured tissue paper
Comics
Cotton
Cotton wool
Crayons
Cup
Dowels or sticks
Drawing pins
Egg-cup
Felt pens
Flower catalogues
Flowery doily
Glitter
Glue
Lacy doily

Lids of all sizes
Lolly stick
Newspapers
Old greeting cards (all kinds)
Packet of star shapes
Paste and brush
Pencil
Pinking shears
Plain postcards
Poster colours
Pretty wallpaper
Punch for holes
Round cheesebox
Ruler
Saucer
Scissors
Scraps
Sellotape
Thin white card
Tooth brushes
Tracing paper
Watercolours
White and black
   cartridge papers
White embossed wallpaper
White gummed paper
Wire paper clips

FOLD AND CUT STRIPS FOR EASTER

Materials: a. Yellow cartridge paper for chicken
           b. Grey cartridge paper for rabbit
           c. Colour or felt pens
           d. Pencil   e. Scissors
           f. Ruler   g. Paste

1. Cut a strip of yellow paper 30cm x 9cm (11.5" x 3.5"), fold in half and crease.

2. Fold in half again by bending the top half backwards, and do the same with the bottom half, concertina-fashion, leaving two folds on the left and two edges on the right. Doing this makes it easier for cutting.

3. Draw this chicken outline on the top fold. Notice that the beak, breast and grass touch the two folds side, and the tail and the grass touch the one fold and two edges side.

4. Cut round the outline carefully. DO NOT CUT AWAY THE FOLDS WHERE PARTS OF THE CHICKEN AND GRASS TOUCH THEM. Save the bits marked 'X'.

5. Open out. Does yours look like this?

6. a.b. Put the pieces marked 'X' in 4, above, together. Lay them down
   c. with the straight edge at the bottom as in (a). You can see that the curve at the top looks like a wing, so draw another curve below it (b) then cut out the four wings together.

7. Lay the chicken strip out flat. Put a little paste on the rounded part of the wing only, and stick to the chicken's body at 'X' and 'X'. Be sure to put them the right way up. Draw in the eyes. Colour the beaks orange, and make green lines for the grass.

8. Refold the chickens and write Easter Greetings on the front one.

9. a.b. The rabbit is made in the same way, but using grey paper 16cm
   c. x 8cm (6.5" x 3.25") folded as in 1, 2 and 3, above. Draw the rabbit and cut out as in 4, above. Then colour the grass and write the greetings.

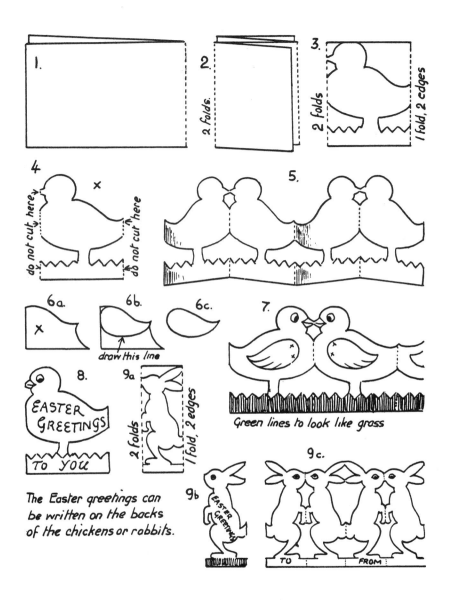

1.

2. 2 folds.

3. 2 folds. 1 fold, 2 edges

4. do not cut here ✗ do not cut here

5.

6a. ✗

6b. draw this line

6c.

7. Green lines to look like grass

8. EASTER GREETINGS TO YOU

9a. 2 folds 1 fold, 2 edges

9b. EASTER GREETINGS

9c. TO FROM

The Easter greetings can be written on the backs of the chickens or rabbits.

11

FOLD AND CUT STRIPS FOR CHRISTMAS

Materials: a. White cartridge paper   b. Green cartridge paper
                    c. Colours   d. Scissors
                    e. Ruler   f. Pencil

1. a.b. This is made in a similar fashion to the folded chicken. The paper used is 20cm x 9cm (12" x 3.5"). Fold this in half and crease (a). Fold in half again by bending the top over on to the fold, and the bottom one backwards to the fold, concertina fashion (b).

2. Fold in half again in the same way, bending the side with the two folds over on to the one fold and two edges side. This will give you three folds and two edges on the left and two thick folds on the right.

3. Draw this half figure of an angel with the wings and lower part of the skirt on the folds as you see here.

4. Cut round the drawn lines, but NOT where any part touches any fold.

5. a.b. Open out and you will find that you have four angels. If you want only three angels, cut one off, but don't throw it away, save it. Refold the last angel so that her wings come forward like the others. Draw in the angels' faces, hair, hands and wings. Colour them. Write your greetings on the books that the angels are holding (b).

6. Now make a single card with the angel you cut off. Cut a strip of card 15cm x 9cm (6" x 3.5"), fold in half and paste the angel on the front and colour it. Cut a greeting from an old card and paste inside.

7. a.b. These trees are folded in the same way and in the same size of paper, but using green paper this time.

8. a.b. The puddings are done in exactly the same manner in white paper, and then coloured.

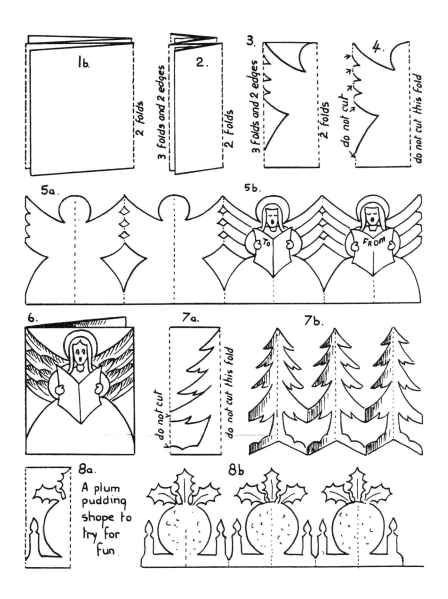

1b.

2 folds

3 folds and 2 edges

2.

2 Folds

3.

3 folds and 2 edges

V V V

2 folds

do not cut

4.

do not cut this fold

5a.

5b.

To

FROM

6.

7a.

do not cut

do not cut this fold

7b.

8a.

A plum pudding shape to try for fun.

8b

13

FOLDED STRIP FOR EASTER

Materials: a. Brown cartridge paper
             b. Green cartridge paper   c. Yellow cartridge paper
             d. Scissors   e. Ruler
             f. Paste   g. Pencil

1. Cut a strip of brown paper 21cm x 10cm (8.25" x 4") and fold in half.

2. Fold in half again by bending the top piece forward on to the fold, and the underneath piece backwards to the fold.

3. Fold in half again in the same way, by bending the two fold sides over on to the one fold and two edges side.

4. Rule this cross on the top fold. Notice that the arm of the cross is twice as wide as the centre strip. This is because when the paper is unfolded the centre will then be the same width as the cross-bar.

5. a.b. Cut out the cross, but not where the arm and mound touch the
c. fold (a). Open out to find that you have cut four crosses (b). As there were only three crosses on Calvary, cut one off to be used as a single card.

6. a.b. Lay the crosses flat on to a strip of green paper the length of three crosses (a). Draw round the outline of the mounds with a pencil and cut them out in one strip (b).

7. Very carefully paste the green strip over the brown mounds at the foot of the crosses. Refold all the crosses so that the arms bend forward. Write your greetings on the mounds.

Make a single card with the cut-off cross.

8. Cut a strip of yellow paper about 12cm x 16cm (5" x 6.5"). Fold it in half and paste the cross on the front, leaving the inside for your greetings and Easter message.

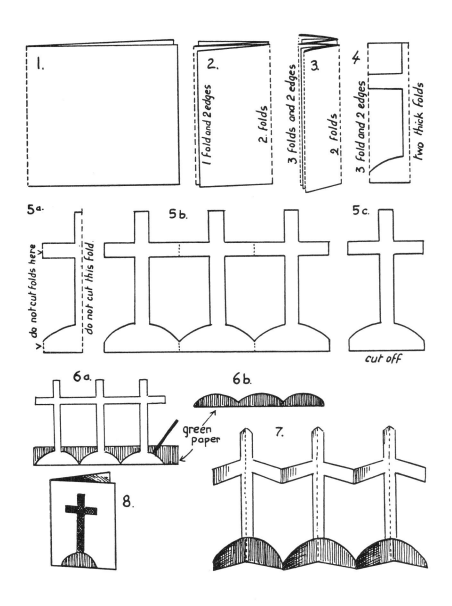

1.

2. 1 fold and 2 edges / 2 folds

3. 3 folds and 2 edges / 2 folds

4. 3 fold and 2 edges / two thick folds

5a. do not cut folds here / do not cut this fold

5b.

5c. cut off

6a. green paper

6b.

7.

8.

SIMPLE FOLD CARDS

Materials: a. Coloured cartridge papers
             b. Old greetings cards
             c. Magazines   d. Flower catalogues
             e. Scissors   f. Ruler
             g. Colours   h. Paste

The size of these cards will depend upon the pictures you are going to use. Here are several, all cut from old cards and magazines and flower catalogues.

First method:

1. The paper for the card is folded, but not quite in half.

2. a.b. The picture is cut from an old card. It is cut straight up where it will lie along the fold then around the outline of the figure or plants or buildings on the right hand side, as shown by the heavy black line (a). This cut-out picture is then pasted on the half flap of the folded card (b).

Second method:

3. Really just the same except that the paper for the card is folded exactly in half and the top flap folded back in half again. It is on this folded back half that the picture is pasted.

4. a.b. Flowers from catalogues are usually on thin paper, so are pasted
c. completely over the top half of the folded card (a). The edge by the fold is trimmed straight, and the card itself is cut round the flower outline on the right hand side (b). On the card in (c) the pot of flowers was pasted first on to a piece of paper of the same colour as the card. The whole thing was then cut out and pasted on to the folded back flap (c).

Third method:

5. Fold back the top flap of this card, crease, and open the card flat. Draw a shape, or paste your picture, in the centre of the left-hand flap, with the crease running through the centre of the design (a.b.c.). Using very sharp scissors, carefully cut round the right-hand side of the design, stopping at the crease as shown by the heavy black line. Refold the card along the centre crease, but NOT the picture, which will stand out (d.e.f.).

1.

2ᵃ. Cut away from old card here cut off

cut out here ↗

2ᵇ.

3. fold not cut

Top page for this card is folded back in half and picture stuck on

4ᵃ.

4ᵇ.

4ᶜ.

5ᵃ.

5ᵇ.

5ᶜ.

5d

5ᵉ.

5f.

TWO-FOLD EASTER CARD

Materials: a. Coloured cartridge papers
               b. Pink, white, red, and yellow gummed paper
               c. Ruler
               d. Scissors
               e. Pencil

This can be made in any size, using paper roughly three times as long as its width.

1.   This card was made from a strip 25cm x 8cm (10" x 3.25"), folded into three equal sections.

2.   Bend back in half the two outside pages and crease so that their folds meet in the centre. .

3. a.b. Measure the width of the two flaps A and B when closed. Cut two pieces of pink gummed paper about 1cm (.5") less than this width. Put these together, folded in half (a) and cut out a half oval shape. These are for the eggs (b).

4.   Stick the left half only of one egg to the left-hand flap so that its crease is over the fold. Stick the right half of the other egg to the right-hand flap so that its crease lies over the fold, too, but make sure that when the flaps are closed both halves of the egg come together in the centre. On each half egg which is not yet stuck down, cut out a little to make it look like broken eggs.

5. a.b. From yellow gummed paper cut two chicken heads and a little part of the body, and stick behind the broken eggshells. Cut beaks from red gummed paper to stick on, and draw in their eyes.

6.   Lay the card down opened flat and stick the half eggs with their chicken heads to the inside half of the flaps. Add little bits cut from the discarded pieces of egg to look like broken eggshell.

7. a.b. For the centre of the card cut a piece of white paper to fit the
   c.   centre, fold in half and cut this simple design (a) round its edges. Open out and stick in the centre of the card. Write on it your 'Easter Greetings', or cut them from old cards and stick on.

8.   Refold the card with both halves together so that the eggs look like one whole egg.

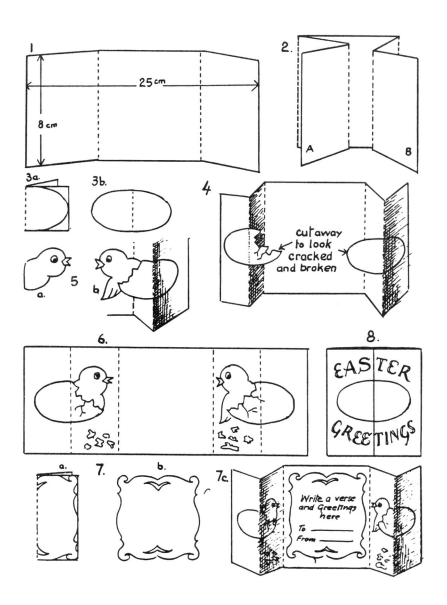

1

25 cm

8 cm

2.

A   B

3a.

3b.

4   cutaway
to look
cracked
and broken

5   a.   b.

6.

7.   a.   b.

7c.   Write a verse
and Greetings
here

To ———
From ———

8.

EASTER

GREETINGS

THREE-FOLD CARDS FOR OTHER OCCASIONS

Materials: a. Coloured cartridge papers   b. White gummed paper
                     c. Coloured gummed papers   d. Scissors
                     e. Pinking shears   f. Felt pens
                     g. Paste and brush   h. Pencil and ruler

1. All these cards are folded in exactly the same way as on the previous page: a long strip folded in three with the top flaps folded back, with their folds meeting in the centre.

2. a.b. The Christmas trees are cut out from green gummed paper.

    c. Measure one of the flaps when opened out, and cut two pieces the same size. Fold in half. The half tree is drawn on it from the fold, and each piece is cut out (a). Stick these carefully over the crease in each flap (b). From a folded piece of white gummed paper, a simple shape is cut out as described on the previous page. This is for your greetings to be written or pasted on. Close the flaps to make a tree (c).

3. a.b. The St. Valentine's card is a white one, with hearts cut from
    c.d. folded red paper (a). Cut two pieces of red the same size, put them together folded and cut the hearts out (b). Stick the hearts over the folded flaps (c) making sure that both come together to meet as one when the flaps are closed (d). Cut another heart for the centre of the card. This could be cut with pinking shears from the folded red paper.

4. a.b A birthday card for a child keen on fishing, made slightly different-
    c. ly, but again on a long strip folded into three. Do not bend back the top flaps yet. Measure the flaps and cut two pieces of green gummed paper the same size. Draw a fish on one of them and cut it out (a). Lay it on the other piece, draw round it and cut that one out too. Put both fish together. Fold in half and crease well. Separate them (b). Now fold back the two flaps on the card, and stick the fish over the crease in each one, so that when the flaps are closed only one fish is seen. The white shape in the centre could be a jam jar (c). Draw bubbles coming from the fishes' mouths.

5. a.b. A card for a grown-up angler. Fold the strip into three again and bend back the top flaps. Keep the flaps closed, and on them draw a fish like (a). Open out the card and lay flat. Continue drawing a long body right across the centre of the card from side to side, joining the lines up at head and tail (b).

6. a.b. Another variation for a birthday or even a get-well card. This card is again folded in three. This time draw a head and trumpet like this on the bent back flaps (a). Then open up the card and write your greeting right across the centre of the card, joining up the two halves of the trumpet.

FOLD AND CUT CARD FOR ST. VALENTINE'S DAY

Materials: a. Green cartridge papers
                b. Thin white paper
                c. Red gummed paper
                d. Scraps (bought) or old cards
                e. Blotting paper   f. Scissors
                g. Pinking shears   h. Punch for holes
                i. Paste and brush   j. Felt pens
                k. Newspaper to work on

This card uses green cartridge paper 30cm x 11cm (12" x 4.5") and white paper cut to the same size.

1. a.b. Fold the green paper in half (a) and in half again by bending the top part back to the fold on the left, and the bottom part back to the fold (b). Lay on one side.

2. Fold the white paper in half, and using scissors or pinking shears cut round the edges, but do not cut the fold. Crease and open out to have the crease running down the centre.

3. Bend the fold on the left over on to the middle crease.

4. Now bend the two loose edges over on to that middle crease. Cut two or three simple shapes from the thick fold on the right, but leave parts of the fold uncut between them.

5. One last folding: bend back the loose edges again to rest on the thick fold on the right. Cut two half-heart shapes from the two folds on the left, and punch three small holes in the corners.

6. Open out. Is yours something like this? Open out the green card and carefully paste the white strip on to it so that the three folds of cuts in the white one are exactly over the three folds in the green one. When dry, refold the card into four parts again.

7. a.b.
c. Decorate each fold of the card with a scrap or small picture cut from old cards (c) that suit the occasion. If you want a Valentine, a heart can be cut from a square of red gummed paper folded in half (b). Write a message on the heart (a).

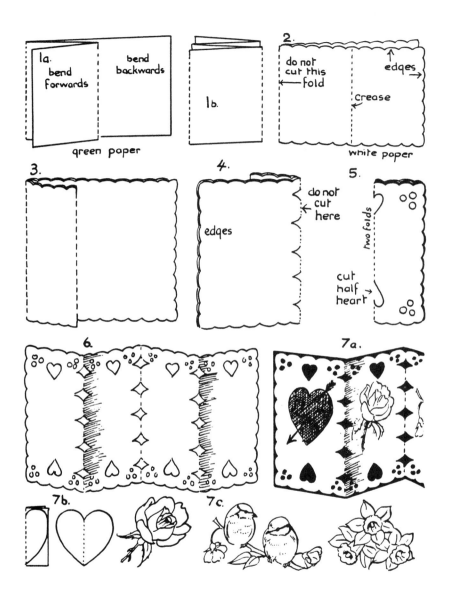

1a. bend forwards   bend backwards

green paper

1b.

2. do not cut this ←fold   edges→   Crease

white paper

3.

4. edges   do not cut here

5. two folds   cut half heart→

6.

7a.

7b.

7c.

23

TWO BELL CARDS

Materials: a. Coloured cartridge papers
             b. White paper   c. Ruler
             d. Scissors   e. Paste

First card:

1. Cut a piece of coloured paper about 15cm x 12cm (6" x 5") and fold in half. Crease and open out. Fold in half again the other way on the same crease. Keep the card folded, and from the fold draw half a bell. Notice that the bell only reaches half-way across the card, and that the rim is not finished off at 'X'–'X'.

2. Cut round the half shape, both sides together, but DO NOT CUT the rim at 'X'–'X'. Make sure that the cuts there stop exactly one above the other. Open out.

3. Hold the card with its centre fold away from you and carefully push the bell forward and out away from the card, closing the card while doing so. This will force the card to crease along the uncut parts of the bell at 'X'–'X'.

4. a.b.
c. Close the card with the bell inside it (a). You can leave it like this, writing the greetings at the side, or cut another piece of paper the same size but of a different colour (b). Put paste round the edge of the card with the bell, but NOT on the bell, and stick the two cards together. When the card is opened the bell will stand forward, showing the other coloured card behind it (c).

Second card:

5. a.b. This card is made the same way as in 1 and 2 (above), but on a slightly wider card, 21cm x 12cm (8" x 5") (a). Before drawing the bell on the fold, the top half of the card is folded back on to the fold, and the bottom half bent backwards and all well creased (b), then re-opened to the half card.

6. The bell is now drawn from the centre fold, but must not reach the crease. The rim stops at 'X'–'X' as in 1 (above). Cut round the outline as in 2 (above), and also cut round the top corners of the card like this. Close the card as in 3 (above) to bring the bell forwards, and crease again.

7.&8. Cut another card of the same size but of a different colour and stick the bell card on to it, but do not stick the bell down. Refold the card with the bell bent forward inside. Then bend the sides of the card back, enabling the card to stand on its own. Round off the corners. The greetings can be written on the side flaps, and on the front of the card when folded.

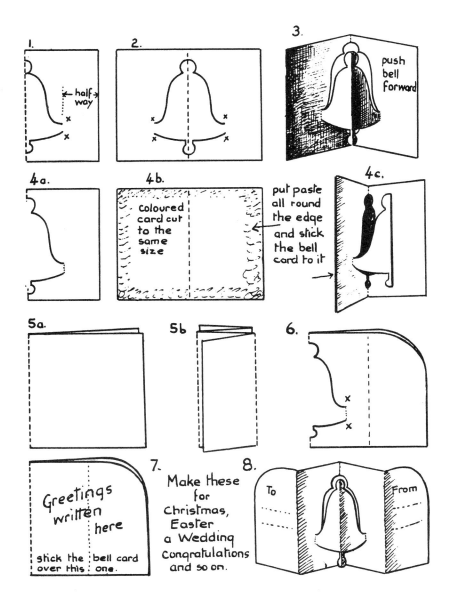

1.

← half →
way

×
×

2.

× ×

× ×

3.

push
bell
forward

4a.

4b.

Coloured
card cut
to the
same
size

put paste
all round
the edge
and stick
the bell
card to it

4c.

5a.

5b.

6.

×
×

7.

Make these
for
Christmas,
Easter
a Wedding
Congratulations
and so on.

Greetings
written
here

stick the bell card
over this one.

8.

To

From

POP-UP CHRISTMAS AND EASTER CARDS

Materials: a. White drawing paper   b. Colours
                   c. Glitter   d. Scissors
                   e. Pinking shears   f. Pencil
                   g. Ruler   h. Paste

1.   Cut the paper to 18cm x 14cm (7" x 5.5"). Fold it in half, crease and open out. Turn the paper over. Recrease the fold from the other side.

2.   Place the fold on your left and bend the top corner down on to the edges and crease. Open up.

3.   Turn the paper over and bend the same corner down again along the same crease. Press and open up.

4.   Measure half way along the top edge and rule a straight line down to the crease.

5.   Make a mark the same distance down from the top on the edges and rule a line across to meet the other on the creases. Cut the square out, both sides together.

6.   Open out. Is your card like this? At this stage make sure the folds are well creased backwards and forwards.

7. a.b.   Hold the paper at the bottom and carefully bend the top part forward and down on to the slanting creases. Press the sides and middle one together (a). When the top is bent right down inside the card, crease firmly again (b).

8.   When the card is opened again the inside part will pop up.

9. a.b.   Open the card and refold it in half, with the top piece up, and on that piece draw the half angel outline of halo and wing tips (a). While still folded, cut round the outline, both sides together (b). Now cut small pieces away from the edges to give a cloud effect.

10.a.b.   Open again and draw in the angel's face, hands and feathers, and then colour them. If using glitter put just a little paste on the wings and halo, and sprinkle a little glitter on them (a) and (b).

11.   Cut a greeting or verse from an old card with pinking shears and paste to the card below the angel on the front, or write your own. Close the card again with the angel inside ready to pop up when opened.

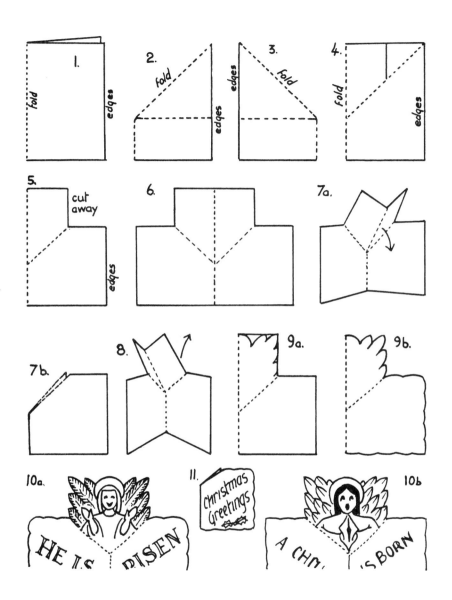

1.

fold

edges

2.

fold

fold

edges

3.

edges

fold

edges

4.

fold

edges

5.

cut away

edges

6.

7a.

7b.

8.

9a.

9b.

10a.

HE IS RISEN

11.

Christmas Greetings

10b

A CHRIST IS BORN

POP-UP CARDS FOR OTHER OCCASIONS

Materials: a. White or coloured cartridge paper
                 b. Old greeting cards and other pictures
                 c. Flower catalogue   d. Tracing paper
                 e. Scissors   f. Paste
                 g. Pencil and white crayon   h. Colours

These are made from old cards and pictures exactly as the angel on the previous page, but adapted for other special occasions or for invitation cards. Follow the same instructions for the folding. Remember it is important that the picture you want to pop up must NOT be wider or taller than the cut shape at the top of the card, so when it is folded and closed, no part of it can be seen beyond the edges of the card itself.

1. a.b. Fold and cut the card as for the angel (a). Lay the top part of the card over the picture that you intend to use, and draw round it (b). Tracing off the square shape with its slanting folds and then laying it over the picture first will help you centre the subject before cutting. It does not matter if the picture goes over the slanting folds a little, but the card will then need to be refolded and recreased very firmly. Trim the card neatly round the picture.

2. a.b. A few ideas using pictures from old cards and a flower catalogue.
c.d. The St. Valentine's heart is from a square of paper. The width of
e.   the cut part of the card is folded in half and the half heart drawn and cut out (e).

3. a.b This Hallowe'en invitation card is slightly different, but folded in
c.d. the same way. When folded in half, the black paper is almost a square. A strip 23cm x 14cm (9" x 5.5") becomes 11.5cm x 14cm (4.5" x 5.5") when folded. Bend the corner on the fold down over on to the edges and crease (a). Open out and bend down again on the other side and crease. Open again to form the half card. A drawing of a half bat figure, with outspread wings, is drawn from the fold with the points of the wings touching the slanting creases (b). Cut round the bat's ears and top of the wings first, then right down along the crease from A to B. Do NOT cut between B and C. Finally make the lower part of the wings (c). Refold to have the bat inside. Write 'Invitation To' on the outside, with a witch's cauldron for atmosphere. The rest of the invitation, time and dress is written inside, to be revealed when the card is opened (d).

Greetings and other wording for all cards can be either written neatly or cut from old cards and pasted in.

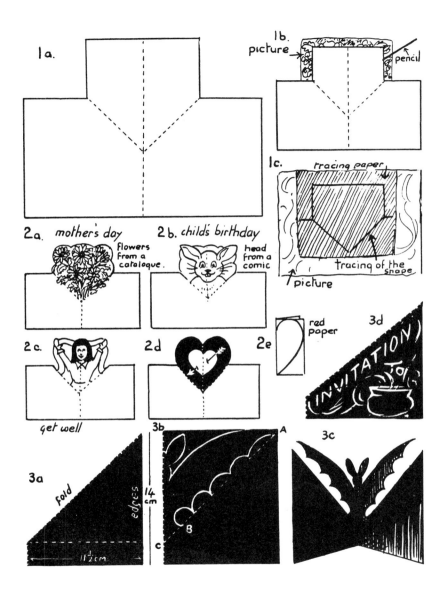

1a.

1b. picture — pencil

1c. tracing paper — tracing of the shape — picture

2a. mother's day — flowers from a catalogue.

2b. child's birthday — head from a comic

2c. get well

2d.

2e. red paper

3a. fold — edges — 14 cm — 11½ cm

3b. A — B — C

3c.

3d. INVITATION To

'OPEN-DOORS' FOR ALL OCCASIONS

Materials: a. Coloured cartridge paper
            b. Old greeting cards   c. Scissors
            d. Paste   e. Pencil

These cards were made from sheets of coloured paper 19cm x 25cm (7.5" x 10").

1.   Fold the paper in half.

2.   And in half again.

3.   Draw the outline of a door on the top page. Make two cuts to allow the door to open, one from the bottom upwards and the other across the top of the door to reach the other drawn line.

4.   Carefully open the door, and with a pencil lightly draw round the open space on to the paper beneath.

5. a.b. Open the paper fully and lay the card flat in front of you. Select a suitable picture for the occasions, which should be large enough to cover the pencil line, and stick it down (a). Put paste all round the page with the door cut in it, but NOT on the door itself (b). Close the card and press down well, leaving the door open!

6.   Refold the card, draw in the panels on the door, the knocker, the letter box and the handle. Make a small slit in the letter box, insert a small piece of paper and stick the end inside the door. On the outside of the paper write 'pull'. Close the door. When the door is pulled open the picture is seen inside.

7. a.b. Here are different types of doors. 7(c) is a stable door which can
c.d. be cut in half so that each half opens separately. 7(d) is cut like a rock to open for Easter.

8.   A little different again. The drawn door is cut down the centre and along the top so that two half doors are opened to show the stable scene inside.

The greetings can be written on the inside of the door, or cut from an old card and pasted on.

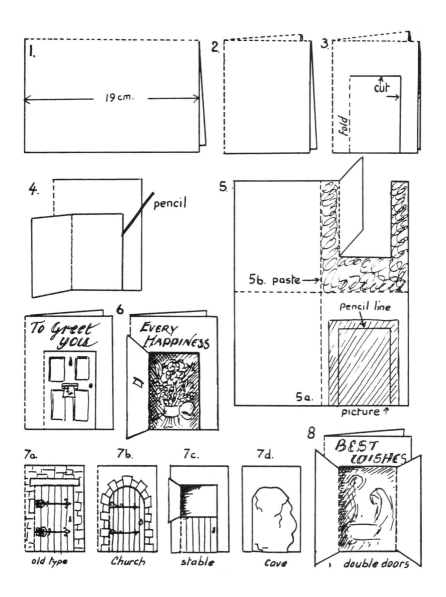

1.

← 19 cm. →

2.

3.

cut

fold

4.

pencil

5.

5b. paste →

Pencil line

5a.

picture ↑

6.

To Greet you

EVERY HAPPINESS

7a.

old type

7b.

Church

7c.

stable

7d.

Cave

8

BEST WISHES

double doors

31

CARDS FOR ANY OCCASION

Materials: a. Coloured cartridge paper
              b. Old Christmas cards
              c. Bought scraps etc.   d. Cup or lid
              e. Scissors   f. Pinking shears
              g. Ruler   h. Paste
              i. Cotton   j. Pencil

These cards, as you see, can be made for any occasion, all made in a single folded card in any size.

1. Fold the card in half, and open out. With the help of the ruler, measure a square or oblong in the centre of the left-hand page, leaving a slightly larger margin at the bottom. Cut out the shape cleanly.

2. a.b. Look through your old cards and cut out any small picture, motif, figure, animal, bird, flower, cottage, etc. to use for these cards, in a size suitable to fit inside the shape cut in the card. Select the small picture for the card and lay it face down on the table. Make sure that it is the right way up. Cover the back of the picture with paste. Lay the end of a small length of cotton down the centre (a). Cover it with a piece of paper the same size as the picture, or cover it with another small picture, also of the same size (b).

3. a.b. Cut a small strip of paper the same colour as the card. Lay the picture in the centre of the hole cut in the card and anchor the cotton to the top of the card with the small strip (a) and (b). The small picture should hang and swing neatly, so do not have the cotton too long. Trim off the surplus.

4. For certain occasions, different shaped cards can be cut, and different shaped holes cut in the cards. A diamond shape for a diamond wedding, a star for Christmas or Easter, a keyhole for a 21st birthday. The lid of a jar or a small box or other shaped object can be put on the card, drawn round and then cut out.

If you use pictures cut from magazines or thin paper, it is best to strengthen them by sticking them on to another piece of paper first. The pictures may be cut with pinking shears to give a fancy edge. The greetings go inside the card, either written or pasted in from an old card.

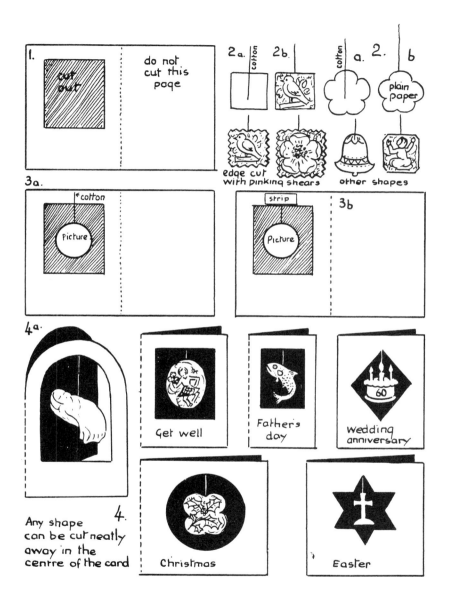

1. cut out

do not cut this page

2a. cotton **2b.** cotton **a. 2.** b

plain paper

edge cut with pinking shears

other shapes

3a. cotton Picture

strip **3b** Picture

4a. Any shape can be cut neatly away in the centre of the card

4.

Get well

Fathers day

wedding anniversary

Christmas

Easter

FLORAL CARDS
MOTHER'S DAY – GET WELL

Materials: a. White or pale coloured cartridge paper
          b. Brown cartridge paper   c. White gummed paper
          d. Doily   e. Flower catalogues
          f. Scissors   g. Paste and brush
          h. Ruler   i. Pinking shears
          j. Small lid or cup   k. Wallpaper

1. Cut a piece of green or pale coloured cartridge paper 30cm x 11cm (12" x 4.5") and fold in half. Measure 3cm (1.25") from the bottom of the top page and rule a line across.

2. a.b. c. A piece of pretty wallpaper, or coloured paper, can be used for the vase. Fold a piece 7cm x 4 cm (2.75" x 1.5") in half (a). Draw this half vase shape (b) and cut out (c).

3. Cut a strip of brown paper 11cm x 3cm (4.5" x 1.25") and paste across the bottom of the card where you ruled the line to represent the table top. Cut the corner off a lacy doily to stick on the table, or cut a small triangle with pinking shears, to look like a table mat. Paste the vase in the centre on the table mat.

4. a.b. Cut out flowers and leaves from an old flower catalogue (a). Arrange these attractively over the vase, allowing some to overlap the edge of the vase. When satisfied, carefully paste them into position (b). Write your words of greeting on the bottom of the card, or cut suitable ones from an old card.

5. a.b. Another attractive card. Fold a 30cm (12") square of coloured paper in half (a) and in half again to make a smaller square (b).

6. a.b. Find a cup, lid or some other circular object 6cm to 7 cm (2.5" to 2.75") across. Place this on white gummed paper, draw round it and cut it out (a). Stick this to the centre of the top page of the card (b).

7. Arrange cut-flowers and leaves all around this circle overlapping the edge to make an attractive garland. Stick carefully into place. Write a simple greeting in the centre, and inside write 'To' and 'From' and your best wishes.

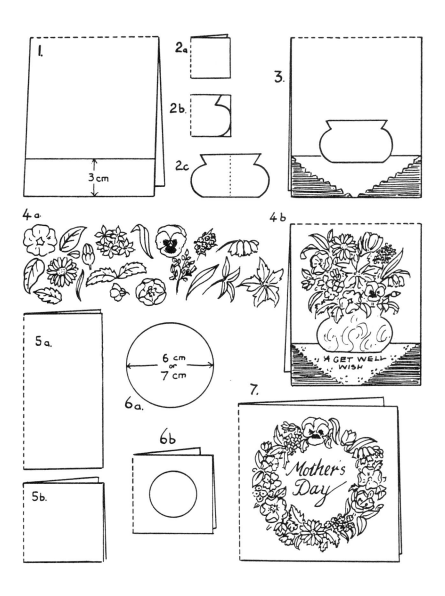

1.

2a.

2b.

3.

2c.

3 cm

4 a.

4 b.

5 a.

6 cm
or
7 cm

6 a.

A GET WELL
WISH

7.

6 b.

Mother's
Day

5 b.

FLORAL CARDS

Materials: a. White cartridge paper
             b. Green cartridge paper
             c. Small piece of yellow paper
             d. Flower catalogue   e. Colours
             f. Scissors   g. Pencil
             h. Paste and brush   i. Ruler

1.   A long strip of white cartridge paper 30cm x 12cm (12" x 5") is folded in half to make a tall card.

2.   Fold in half again lengthways.

3.   Draw a half flower and leaf with its centre on the fold, the flower pot and base. This base should be as least 2cm (1") deep.

4.   Cut neatly round the outline, but only the half-heart shape from the centre of the flower on the fold. Do not make the stem too long or thin.

5.   Cut two strips of green paper 12cm (5") long and as wide as the base you have cut. Paste these on the bottom of the card on the back and front strips.

6.   Colour the flower, leaves and pot, and leave to dry quite flat under a weight. When dry, open the card and lay it face down. Cut a small piece of yellow paper and stick over one heart-shaped hole. Then put paste all over the other flower head only. Close the card and press well so that the flower heads are stuck together.

7.   Write your greetings on the green base and open up the card so that it stands on its own.

8. a.b. In some flower catalogues you will find lovely pots of flowers
    c.   that can be treated in the same way. First cut them out roughly round their outline (a) and paste on to a folded card, leaving a strip below the pot for the base (b). When quite dry, cut round the outline of the plant or flowers, cutting both halves together. As only the front of the card has a picture on it, the back can be left plain for your message. Add just a little paste in between the flower heads to make the card stand more firmly.

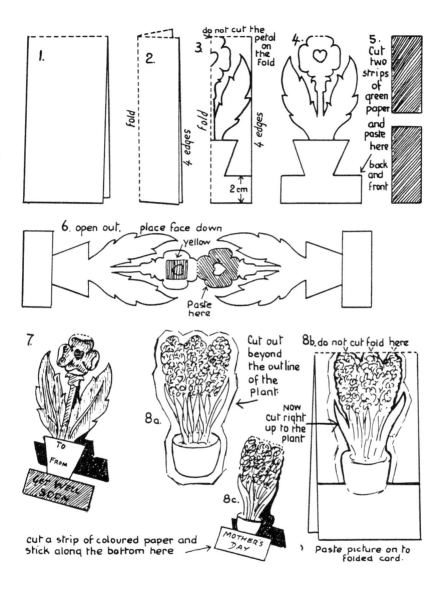

1.

2. fold

3. do not cut the petal on the fold
fold
4 edges
2 cm

4.

5. Cut two strips of green paper and paste here
back and front

6. open out. place face down
yellow
Paste here

7. TO
FROM
GET WELL SOON

cut a strip of coloured paper and stick along the bottom here

8a. Cut out beyond the outline of the plant

Now cut right up to the plant

8b. do not cut fold here

8c. MOTHER'S DAY

Paste picture on to folded card.

FLORAL CUT-OUT CARD

Materials: a. Flower catalogue
                b. Coloured cartridge paper
                c. White cartridge paper
                d. Narrow ribbon or cord
                e. Scissors
                f. Paste
                g. Pencil

1. a.b.
c.d. Search through old flower catalogues for pictures of large flower heads, or bunches of small heads like these (a.b.c.d.). Cut them from the catalogue, but NOT round their outline yet (a). Measure the flower head in both directions, and cut a strip of coloured paper, the width being at least the same as the height of the flower head and its length as least twice its width. The pansy here was 7cm across, so a strip of paper 14.5cm long by 7cm wide (6" x 3") was used. Fold the strip in half and open out. Paste the flower head on the right-hand side, so that the petals touch the crease in the middle, or even go over it slightly (b).

2. When quite dry refold the card. Holding it carefully, cut round the outline, both sides together, DO NOT CUT THE FOLD on the left, where the flower touches it, or wraps round the back of the card.

3. Cut a strip of white paper the same length and width as the coloured strip in **1** (above). Fold the strip in half, put it inside the flower head, with its fold tight up against the fold in the card. Hold the card and paper firmly on the table and draw round the flower head. Remove the white paper and cut out round the line, both sides together.

4. Cut a short length of narrow ribbon and tie the two pages together, or, if you prefer, put a little paste along the fold of the bottom white page and stick them together.

5. Now you can write your greetings inside.

This makes an ideal 'Get Well' card.

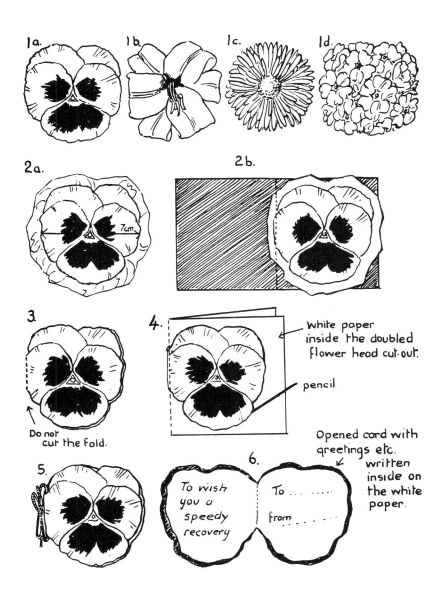

1a.

1b.

1c.

1d.

2a.

7cm

2b.

3.

Do not
cut the fold.

4.

White paper
inside the doubled
flower head cut out.

pencil

5.

6.

To wish
you a
speedy
recovery

To ....

from ......

Opened card with
greetings etc.
written
inside on
the white
paper.

A CANDLE FOR ANY OCCASION

Materials: a. Greetings cut from old cards
            b. White card   c. Colours
            d. Ruler   e. Scissors
            f. Pinking shears   g. Egg-cup

This could do for a birthday or even a wedding anniversary, with the appropriate number of years written on the card. It is especially suitable for Christmas and Easter.

1. a.b. Cut the card 18cm x 11cm (7.25" x 4.5"). Fold it into three
c.d. equal parts. If you find this difficult to do, cut the paper a little
e. wider 18cm x 14.5cm (7.25" x 5.75") (a). Fold in half (b), fold in half again (c), crease and open out. This will give you four equal sections (d). Cut one off which will leave you with three (e).

2. a.b. Recrease the two folds and open out (a). At the top of the middle section put the egg-cup so that it touches the top edge of the paper and goes over the folds on either side. Draw round it, and make two curved lines like this, from the drawn circle out to the sides (b).

3. a.b. Cut around the circle and the two curved lines. Draw a short black line for the candle wick and add the flame. Below this draw a slight curve for the top of the candle (a). If you are able to use pinking shears carefully, the circle round the flame can be cut with them, but not the two curved lines below (b).

4. The candle itself can be left with straight sides, or lines drawn across from crease to crease like this. Draw on a stand for the candle at the bottom. The greetings can be put on the side strips. Colour the candle and its stand.

5. If you do draw lines on the candle, turn the card over and draw similar ones on each of the side strips. Write 'To' and 'From' in the centre space, and colour.

6. a.b. Turn the card over and fold the two side flaps over the centre one. This will make a single candle shape, and on being opened will reveal the greetings. If it is for a birthday, write the appropriate number of years on the candle itself or write on gummed paper and stick on.

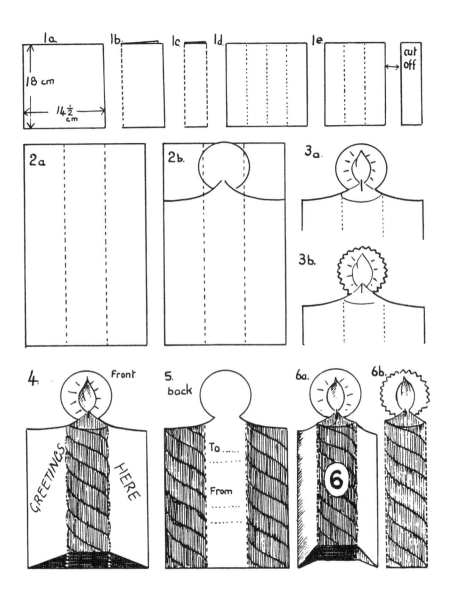

1a. 18 cm, 14½ cm

1b.

1c.

1d.

1e. cut off

2a.

2b.

3a.

3b.

4. Front — GREETINGS HERE

5. back — To..... From.....

6a. 6

6b.

41

PIG'S HEAD INVITATION CARD

Materials: a. Pink cartridge paper
                b. Black felt pen

Any size of square may be used for a pig's head. This one was 15cm (6").

1.   Fold the square corner to corner and crease well.

2.   Open out and crease again on the other two corners.

3.   Bend the bottom corner up 2cm (.75") to make the pig's snout.

4.   Bend down corner 'A' a little way from the middle crease, so that the edges lie straight together.

5.   Repeat with corner 'B'.

6.   Now bend back each point 'A' and 'B' to make the ears. Draw in the nostrils and eyes.

7.   Bend the snout back down again, and using a blunt point (a used ballpoint) press down along the centre crease, from the crease across, down to the tip of the snout. This will make it easier to push the mouth open later on.

8.   Open the card, and write your invitation between the creases as you see here, but not so low as to show when the card is refolded.

9.   Refold carefully to make the pig's head again.

On the back of the card write 'Hold my head behind each ear between finger and thumb, and push together to make my mouth open'. This will then reveal your message inside the head.

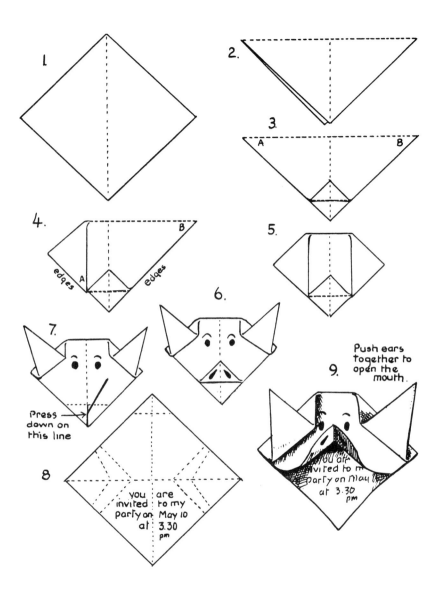

1.

2.

3.
A   B

4.
B
edges   A   edges

5.

6.

7.
Press down on this line

8.
you are invited to my party on May 10 at 3.30 pm

9.
Push ears together to open the mouth.

you are invited to my party on May 10 at 3.30 pm

43

CHILDREN'S PARTY INVITATION

Materials: a. White or coloured cartridge paper
            b. Black felt pen   c. Ruler
            d. Scissors   e. Pencil

Made from a square about 23cm (9") on a side.

1.   Fold in half corner to corner and open up. Fold again on the other two corners and open out.

2.   Fold in half across the paper both ways, crease and open out. Turn over, and recrease the last two folds again, but not the first ones.

3.   When opened out the creases should look like this.

4.   Refold the paper in half and bend the corner at 'X' forward and down on the centre crease.

5.   Bend the corner at 'Y' under backwards on to the centre crease again.

6.   Finally, fold the left-hand triangular half right over on to the right-hand side, and crease well.

7. a.b. Measure 5cm (2") up from the bottom edge and rule a line right
   c.   across the card (a). Draw the teddy bear's head and half shape up to the drawn line. Cut this out carefully (b). Of course, you can draw anything else that might come to mind, like this clown's head (c).

8.   Open out with care, fill in the eyes and nose of the teddy bear. Write your message in the four triangles above the head.

9.   To make the invitation stand up, recrease each fold separately, making sure that each long fold is bent forwards and the short ones, between the heads, bent backwards.

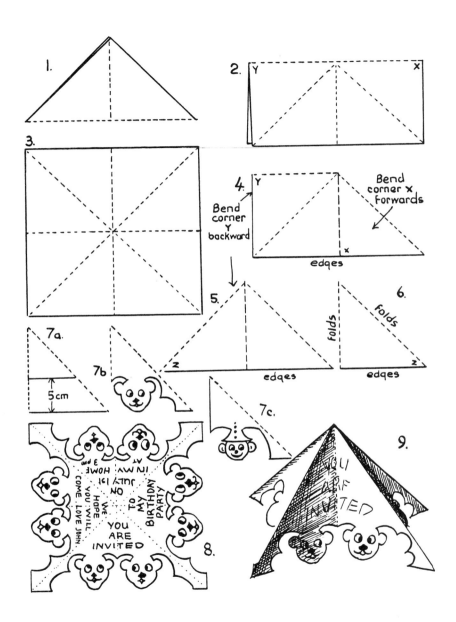

1.

2. Y X

3.

4. Y — Bend corner Y backward — Bend corner X forwards — x — edges

5. edges

6. folds folds edges z z

7a. 5cm

7b.

7c.

8. COME LOVE JOHN. YOU WILL HOPE WE ON JULY 1st IN MY HOME AT 3 pm TO MY BIRTHDAY PARTY YOU ARE INVITED

9. YOU ARE INVITED

CARDS WITH 'STAINED GLASS' EFFECT

Materials: a. Black paper
            b. White paper
            c. Coloured tissue papers
            d. Scissors
            e. Paste and brush
            f. White crayon

These can be any size or shape.

1. Fold the black paper in half to make a double card. Open out.

2. a.b. Using the white crayon, draw this simple shape of a candle or two candles on the left-hand page (a). These shapes are then cut out, but before you start cutting, notice that each part of the candle, the flame, the candle itself and the stand is cut out separately, with a strip of black paper between them, to look like the lead in stained-glass windows.

3. a.b.
c. Cut small pieces of tissue paper to cover each part of the candle, yellow for the flame, red for the candle and green for its base (a), or one red and one green candle on a brown base (b). Be sure not to let one colour overlap on to any other cut-out part of the design. The two candles should look like this from the front (c).

4. Cut a folded piece of white paper slightly smaller than the card to fit inside it. Put paste on the page with the cut-outs on it, but not on the tissue, and stick one side of the folded white card carefully over it. Add your greetings, either writing them in or using those from an old card.

5. Here are some simple Christmas and Easter shapes to try. Can you think of others to do?

4. This page is pasted round the edges only.

WRITE GREETINGS HERE

'STAINED GLASS' FOR MANY OCCASIONS

Materials: a. Black or coloured cartridge paper
                  b. White paper
                  c. Tracing paper
                  d. Scissors
                  e. Pencil
                  f. Paste and brush

Here are a few more suggestions for simple 'stained glass' cards all made in the same way as on the previous page, but using dark blue, brown, green, etc. instead of black paper, if you wish.

1. a.b. A simple flower for Mother's Day, Birthday, Get Well or
   c.d. Anniversary. Draw the simple shape in pencil on the inside of the card. If you find petal and leaf shapes difficult to draw, fold small pieces of paper in half, draw the half shape and cut out. These cut-out shapes can be used as templates to draw round (c). Try creating your own shapes to draw and cut out (d).

2. a.b. Here is a Golden Wedding Anniversary card (a). When drawing
    c. any numbers inside the card, remember they must be drawn backwards. Leave a strip of uncut paper between the inside and outside circles of the 'O' (b). It might help you to draw the numbers on tracing paper first, then turn the tracing pencil-side down inside the card and trace off.

3. Other suggestions for you to try.

1a. 1b. 1c. 1d.

2a. 2b. 2c.

3.

Good voyage

Christening

New home

Child's birthday

Wedding anniversary

These can be cut in black paper or dark coloured paper. Cut each piece separately. Remember to leave a strip of paper between each cut piece.

49

'STAINED GLASS' FROM OLD GREETING CARDS

Materials: a. Old greetings cards of all kinds
                  b. Coloured cartridge paper
                  c. White paper
                  d. Black indian ink or paint and brush
                  e. Small scissors
                  f. Pencil
                  g. Paste and brush
                  h. Newspaper to work on

1. a.b Look through your cards and pick out those which have good
    c.   side views of birds, animals or figures, and clear outlines of
objects, candles, lanterns or buildings.

2.   Cut off the back half of the card. Using small, sharp scissors cut
very carefully round the inside of the figure or object. Start by
piercing the centre with the point of the scissors, then cut out
to the outline and round it completely. Do not leave strips of
uncut paper between parts of the figure or object as on the
previous page.

3. a.b. Put the card on newspaper and paint it all over with indian ink
or black paint. Leave it to dry, then give it another coat to get a
surface of intense black without streaks. When dry, place it
under a weight between paper to dry flat. Cut another card
meantime.

4.   Cut and fold cartridge paper the same size as the blackened card.
Put paste all over the back of the cut-out card and stick it to
the front of the folded paper.

5.   Another idea. Cut and fold the coloured paper to make the card,
then trim the black cut-out a little smaller all round than the
card. Paste the back of it and stick it to the centre of the
coloured card so there is a border all round the same colour as
the inside of the cut out.

Greetings are written or pasted inside.

SILHOUETTES

Materials: a. Thin black poster paper
                b. Coloured cartridge paper
                c. Black indian ink and paintbrush
                d. Old greeting cards, magazines, etc.
                e. White paper   f. Scissors
                g. Paste and brush   h. Newspaper
                i. Black ballpoint   j. Calendars with views

Look through old cards, magazines, etc. for shapes to cut out. Figures, animals and birds are best in profile, that is side view. Figures in movement, like skating, dancing or running, with arms and legs held away from the body are excellent, but need very careful cutting. Fold double cards in white ready to paste on silhouettes.

1. When cutting out the shape first of all, cut outside its outline, not on it.

2. a.b. Paste it on black paper picture side up. Let it dry flat.
   c.

3. When quite dry (this is important, otherwise the paper will not cut with a clear, sharp edge) cut round its outline. Then paste it, black side uppermost, on to the white card.

4. When cutting grass, or anything furry like the squirrel's tail here, make a series of small cuts like this around the outline. Whiskers can be added afterwards with pen and ink or a fine ballpoint, as can lines round the heron's feet in 6(b) to represent water.

5. If you cannot get black paper, lay the rough cut out face down on to newspaper and paint it black all over the back using paint or indian ink. Two coats should be used to make a full, deep black. When dry, trim round the outline and paste black side up on to the white card.

6. a.b. After cutting out, this silhouette was pasted on to a white circle
   c. first, before being mounted on to the card (a). A heron pasted on to white card has lines drawn with a fine ballpoint round its legs to suggest water (b). A more unusual effect can be achieved by pasting a silhouette on to a suitable picture or scene and the whole pasted on to the card, like this deer pasted first on to a mountain scene, and then on to a coloured card (c).

7. The opposite effect can be achieved by pasting the cut out on to white paper, cutting it out and mounting it on black or other very dark card, giving a white silhouette.

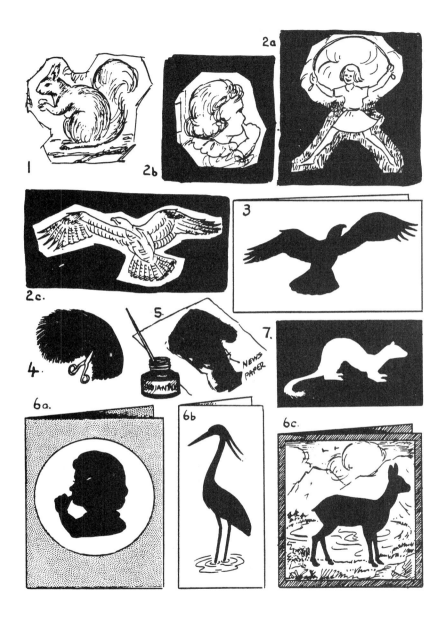

1

2a

2b

2c.

3

4.

5.

NEWS PAPER

7.

6a.

6b

6c.

SPATTER CARDS USING CUT OUTS

Materials:
    a. Coloured or white cartridge paper
    b. Old cards with figures   c. Scissors
    d. Blotting Paper   e. Poster paints
    f. Two used toothbrushes   g. Lid
    h. Lolly-stick   i. Pins   j. Newspaper

Here is something different to try. Look through old cards and select those having a suitable subject with a clear outline to cut out. Buildings, flowers, leaves, figures, animals, any of these with a distinct profile are useful for this purpose. Poster paint, having a little more body than ordinary water colour paint, is best to use, but water colours can be used if mixed thick enough.

1. a.b. Using sharp scissors, pierce the centre of the subject you have chosen (a). Then make small cuts from this centre to the outline and then round the outline itself. This will give a sharp edge to the cut out (b).

2. Cut and fold a card from cartridge paper to fit the cut out. Open it out and lay it on a thick wad of newspaper. Place the cut out on the right-hand page of the card. Push pins into each corner to anchor it as you work. If any part of the cut out stands out from the card, push pins in to hold it down. This will prevent any paint getting under the edge and making a fuzzy line. Cover the left-hand page with more newspaper to keep it clean from the spatter.

3. a.b. Mix the poster paint in the lid. Anything larger is a waste of paint. It should be thickish, like pouring cream (a). Use the two brushes, one to mix the paint, and one to feed the other one (b). Doing it this way can save your work from ugly blobs.

4. a.b. Point the brush you are using for spraying down towards the cut out with the bristles uppermost. With the flat side of the lolly-stick gently stroke the bristles towards you (a). The paint will spray downwards over the cut out. Do not touch the cut-out surface with the brush. More pressure on the bristles will make a heavier spray, but it is really better to spray lightly two or three times to make an even print. If you have cut out several shapes, it is better to spatter them all in turn, and then return to the first and spatter them all again. When satisfied with your spraying, remove all the pins and carefully lift the cut out up and away without smudging the work (b). Blot the cut out dry so that you can use it again.

5. If you are using black or dark coloured paper for your card, spatter with white paint for an interesting variation. Again, wipe the cut out dry for re-use.

A note of caution: do not use worn out toothbrushes where the tufts of bristles are bent over. They will not work efficiently. Do not be tempted to overload the working brush. Wipe the pins after removing from the work, and wash all brushes after use, before storing.

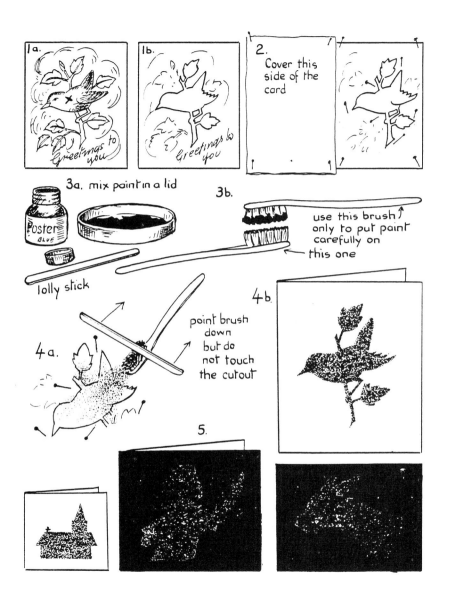

1a.

1b.

Greetings to you

Greetings to you

2. Cover this side of the card

3a. mix paint in a lid

Poster BLUE

lolly stick

3b.

use this brush ↑ only to put paint carefully on ← this one

4a.

point brush down but do not touch the cutout

4b.

5.

SPATTER WITH PRESSED LEAVES

Materials:
   a. Leaves of attractive shapes pressed and dried: ferns are excellent
   b. Plain pale or white cartridge paper
   c. Newspaper to work on
   d. Two toothbrushes   e. Blotting paper
   f. Small pins   g. Poster paints
   h. Tin lids   i. Lolly-stick

Leaves and ferns for this are best gathered in summer. Flowers are not so good, as the petals tend to break, but some umbelliferous seed heads make good prints. Gather those leaves with an attractive shape, and leave the stem on. Arrange them carefully on newspaper. They must not touch each other. Cover with more newspaper, and put a weight on them so that they dry flat for a week or longer if possible. They should be prepared well in advance before using them. The spraying method is similar to that on the previous page. Cut and fold the paper you are using for the cards.

1. a.b. Spread a wad of newspaper down to work on, as it can be a bit messy. Lay the card on the newspaper opened out, and cover the left-hand page with more newspaper (a). Place a leaf or fern on the right-hand side of the card, with its veins uppermost. Push small pins through the tips of the points to keep them flat on the paper (b). If they are not flat on the paper, the paint will creep under the edges and make the print foggy.

2. Mix the paint in the lids to the consistency of pouring cream, and follow the instructions given on the previous page for using the two toothbrushes. Concentrate on spraying the edge of the leaf to make a good contrasting print, but do not overdo it. When satisfied, remove the pins and gently lift the leaf smartly up and away, being very careful not to smudge the wet paint.

3. With practice and care, it is possible to make both a negative and positive print with the same leaf at the same time. Have a second card ready at the side. When you are satisfied that the edge of the leaf has been sprayed enough, spray a little more in the centre if it needs it, but do not make it too wet. When you remove the leaf from the first card, drop it neatly on the second card paint side down. Put blotting paper over it and press very gently with the finger tips all over it. DO NOT thump with the fist as this could cause the leaf to move and spoil the print.

Spattered cards are very attractive and can be used for almost any occasion. The greetings can be written or pasted inside.

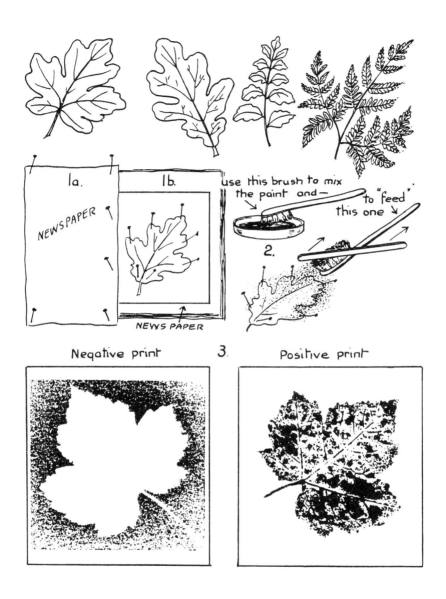

1a.

NEWSPAPER

1b.

NEWSPAPER

use this brush to mix the paint and—

to "feed" this one ↓

2.

Negative print

3.

Positive print

A LARGE LACY VALENTINE

Materials: a. Two lacy doilies
               b. Brown and red gummed paper
               c. A little yellow and black gummed paper
               d. Blue cartridge paper   e. Blotting paper
               f. Scissors   g. Paste and brush
               h. Felt pen   i. Newspaper

1.   This is a much larger card. The doily measured 20cm (8") across. You can make your own doily (see Circular Lacy Cut-outs, page 66). Choose or make one with a plain centre. Measure this plain circle and cut a square of red gummed paper to fit inside it.

2.   For this size of doily the blue paper was cut measuring 42cm x 30cm (16.5" x 11.75"). Fold the paper in half. Place the doily face down on the newspaper and very gently brush paste all over the back of it, or, alternatively, just the centre circle. Lift with care and lay on the card, a little above centre. Cover with blotting paper and smooth down, making sure there are no wrinkles. Put to dry under a weight.

3. a.b. While that is drying, fold the red square (a) in half, red side
   c.   inwards. Draw a half-heart shape (b) and cut out. Open to check the shape (c).

4. a.b. Refold in half, and lightly draw a line about 1cm (.5"), no more,
   c.   from the edge (a). Cut round this pencil line. The result is a smaller heart for the front of the card and another for the inside (b and c).

5.   Stick the first heart in the centre of the doily, and press down with blotting paper.

6.   Open the card and lay it flat. Cut out the centre of the second doily. Paste this on the right-hand page, and stick the second heart on it.

7. a.b. To make the arrow shaft, cut two strips of brown paper about
 c.d. 10cm (4") long (a). Fold a square of yellow paper in half and cut
   e.   this shape for the feathers, making small cuts down the edges (b). Open out and stick one strip of brown paper down the centre (c). Fold a square of black paper in half, and cut it like this (d). Open out and stick it over the end of the other brown strip (e).

8.   Stick these half arrows over the heart and doily inside the card. Draw the curved lines at each end of the brown strips to make the arrow look as though it has pierced the heart.

Your greeting goes on the left-hand page inside the card.

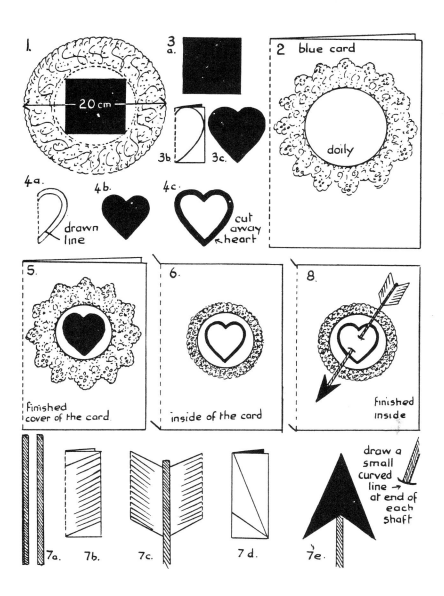

1.

20 cm

3a.

3b. 3c.

2 blue card

doily

4a.

drawn line

4b.

4c.

cut away heart

5.

finished cover of the card.

6.

inside of the card

8.

finished inside

7a. 7b. 7c. 7d.

draw a small curved line → at end of each shaft

7e.

LACY FAN FOR A VALENTINE

Materials: a. Paper doily 20cm (8") across
                b. Short length of white wool or cord
                c. Coloured cartridge paper   d. Red gummed paper
                e. Blotting paper   f. Scissors
                g. Paste and brush   h. Punch for holes
                i. Small two-pronged paper clip j. Felt pen

1. Find a plate or other round object the size of the doily. You can use one slightly larger, but not smaller than the doily. Lay it on the coloured cartridge paper. Draw round it and cut it out. Paste the doily on to this and leave to dry flat under pressure.

2. a.b. Fold the doily and paper in half and crease (a). Fold in half
c. again and crease (b), and in half once more, and crease (c).

3. Open out to find creases like this.

4. Cut along each crease. This will give you eight triangular segments.

5. Lay five triangles on top of one another. Cut off all their points, rounded if possible. With the punch, or sharp pointed scissors, make a small hole through them all. After pushing the paper clip through, open the prongs behind them.

6. Open the fan and write your verse or greeting on the plain centre of each piece.

7. a.b. Twist the white cord, or wool, round the paper clip at the back,
c.d. and cut out small red hearts to stick to the ends. Cut these hearts from four squares of the red gummed paper. Put two together and fold in half (a). Draw and cut out this half heart shape (b). Stick the cord down the centre of one heart (c) and stick another one over it. Do this with the other end (d).

8. a.b. If you do not have a paper clip to hold the ends of the triangles
c. together, bend the cord in half and push the loop through the five segments from the front (a). Bring the loop forward and pass the two ends through it (b). Pull gently to tighten and make firm (c) then stick the hearts on.

Here is a very, very old verse that you might like to write on it for fun:

        Roses are red,
        Violets are blue,
        Sugar is sweet,
        And so are you!

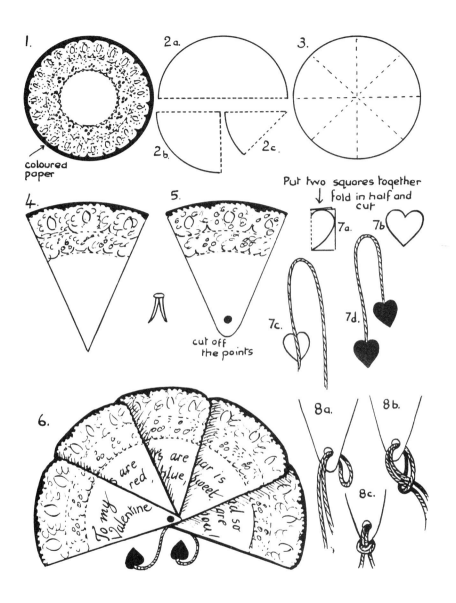

1.

coloured
paper

2 a.

2 b.

2 c.

3.

4.

5.

cut off
the points

Put two squares together
↓ fold in half and
cut

7a.

7b.

7c.

7d.

6.

To my
Valentine

's are
are
red,
blue,
ar is
sweet,
are
so
you!

8a.

8b.

8c.

HEART FOR PARENT'S DAY OR VALENTINE

Materials: a. Thin red card or cartridge paper
              b. White drawing paper
              c. White gummed label   d. Scissors
              e. Glue   f. Pencil

1. Cut four squares in red card and one in white paper. These can be any size, according to the size of card you want.

2. Fold all the squares in half and crease well.

3. Draw this half shape on the white paper and cut it out cleanly. Open it out, and if it is not a good shape, discard it and make another.

4. Place a folded red square in front of you. Put the folded white heart on it with the fold of the heart on the fold of the card, and its top and side touching the top and side of the card beneath. Gently draw round the outline. Repeat this with the other three squares.

5. Cut each heart out carefully. Open to see if they are a good shape.

6. a.b. Refold the red hearts. Place one on the table in front of you. Put glue on the top of the heart only, especially along the fold (a). Pick up the second heart and lay it exactly over the first heart, making sure that the folds, the tops and the sides coincide. Press firmly together. Open it out to check if all is well (b).

7. a.b. Close the second heart and put glue on it. Then stick the third heart exactly over it, as before. You now have three hearts firmly glued together (a). The fourth heart is glued to the third in the same way. To glue them all together, put glue on the back of the fourth heart. Bend the other half of the first heart back, and stick it to the back of the fourth heart, to look like this (b).

8. a.b. Make shapes from the gummed paper as explained in 'Cut out
   c. shapes' (page 70). Stick one to the centre of each heart and write your greeting on them.

For Mother's Day or Father's Day, a suitable small picture such as flowers could be pasted on to one or two of the hearts to make the card more personal.

1. Cut four squares in red

and

one in white

2.

3.

4. white cut out heart on the red paper — pencil

5.

6a first heart put glue on this side — second heart

6b second heart stick this half to first heart — first heart

7a. third heart stick this half to the second heart — second heart

7b. fourth heart

8a.

8b.

8c. cut a different white shape for each heart

FOLDED HEART, MOTHER'S DAY OR VALENTINE

Materials:
    a. Coloured cartridge paper
    b. Red cartridge paper
    c. Doily with a flowery border
    d. Scissors
    e. Paste and brush
    f. Pencil

1. a.b. The size of the card depends upon the size of the doily. The folded card should be slightly larger than the doily, so that there is a border all round the doily. This doily is 16cm (6.5") across, so the paper was cut 18cm x 36cm (7.25" x 14.5") making a square 18cm (7.25") (a). Carefully paste the doily in the centre of the top page of the card (b).

2. a.b. Measure the plain centre of the doily, and cut a piece of red paper twice the width long and once the width wide. This was 7cm (2.75") so it needed a strip 7cm x 14cm (2.75" x 5.5") folded in half (a and b).

3. Fold back the top half of the red paper.

4. Fold back the bottom half of the red paper in the same way, so that you have one fold and two edges on one side, and two folds on the other.

5. On the side of the paper with one fold and two edges draw this half-heart shape. Let the rounded side of the heart come right over on to the side with two folds.

6. Cut round the outline, but do not cut any part that is on a fold. Open out to find one whole heart in the middle and a half heart on each side. Is yours like this?

7. Fold the two halves back to meet in the centre to form one heart.

8. Paste the complete centre heart only to the centre of the doily, leaving the two halves free.

9. Open the two halves and write your greeting on the centre heart.

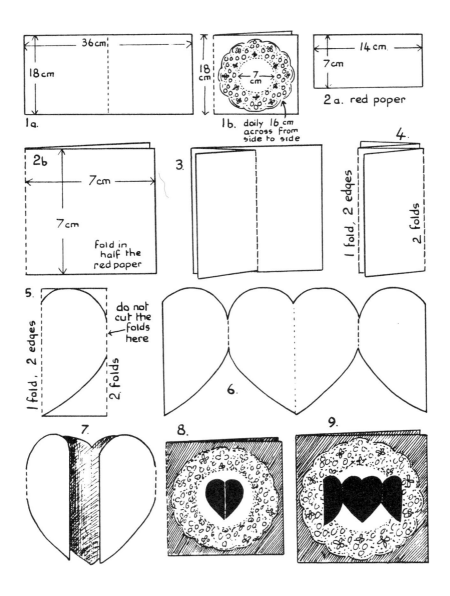

1a. ← 36cm → / 18 cm

1b. ← 7 cm → / 18 cm / doily 16 cm across from side to side

2a. red paper / ← 14 cm → / 7 cm

2b. ← 7cm → / 7cm / fold in half the red paper

3.

4. 1 fold, 2 edges / 2 folds

5. 1 fold, 2 edges / 2 folds / do not cut the folds here

6.

7.

8.

9.

65

CIRCULAR LACY CUT-OUTS

Materials: a. Saucer or side plate
              b. Thin white paper   c. Pinking shears
              d. Jam jar lid   e. Small scissors
              f. Punch for holes   g. Pencil

If you are unable to find suitable lacy doilies for some of the previous cards, try making your own like these. Use a saucer or side plate to draw round for your doily: either should be large enough. Thin white paper, not thick cartridge paper is used for cutting. Tissue paper is too thin and flimsy. Though ideal for many things, it is quite difficult to paste on to the other paper. Try an ordinary uncrumpled white bag for a start.

1. Draw a circle on the white paper, using the plate or saucer as a guide.

2. a.b.
c. Fold the circle in half (a) and in half again so that you have one fold on one edge and two folds on the other (b). Fold once again, but this time bend the top of the two folds over on to the single fold. Turn over and do the same again. ending up with three folds on one side and two on the other (c). Folding in this way makes the later cutting easier.

3. a.b.
c. Place the lid on the top of the triangle so that it touches the top and the edges on either side. Draw round it. If you cut round this with ordinary scissors you will end up with a plain scalloped edge to your doily (a) but if you cut with pinking shears it will give a more interesting edge (b). Or you may cut as in (c), which has been done here in 4, 5, and 6.

4. a.b.
c.d. You can create your own design by cutting away small shapes from the folds. Keep the lower half of the triangle uncut. If you have a punch, use it to make a pattern in the centre near the top (a). If you haven't a punch, make a small simple cut-out shape in the centre. Pierce right through the paper with the point of the scissors (b). Then make small cuts outwards (c). Then cut small snips away (d).

5. Opened out, 4(a) would look like this.

6. a.b. If your paper is thin enough, and you think you could manage it, your paper may be folded once more, backwards and forwards as in 2(c) (above). Then cut away the design (a) which opens out to (b). These are the same shaped cuts as in 4 (above), but smaller.

7. Two more different patterns to try.

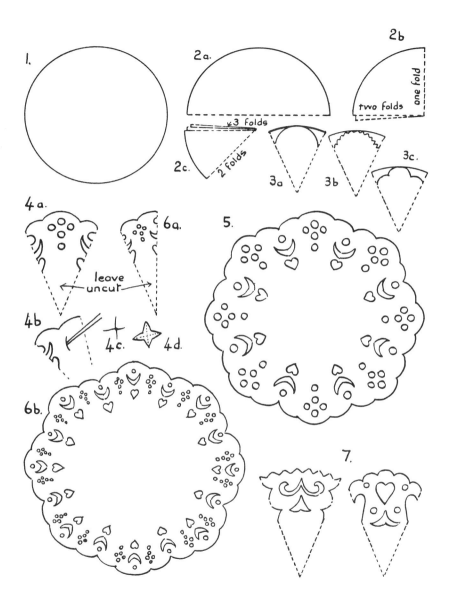

1.

2a.

2b

one fold

two folds

←3 folds

2c.

2 folds

3a

3b

3c.

4a.

6a.

leave
uncut

4b

4c.

4d.

5.

6b.

7.

CUT PAPER WORK

Materials: a. Black, white or coloured cartridge paper
                  b. White or coloured gummed paper
                  c. Blotting paper
                  d. Scissors
                  e. Pencil

This type of card embodies the same kind of idea as the previous page but as you can see the extra folding of the paper can give more interesting designs. When using gummed paper, fold with the gummed side outside and draw your outline on this.

1. a.b. Using white gummed paper, try this Christmas tree first. Fold the paper in half, draw the half tree, leaving a border (a). Opened out it looks like this (b).

2. a.b.
**   c.** Fold another piece of gummed paper in half (a) and half again, bottom to top (b). Draw this tree. Put the point of the scissors through the paper at 'X' and cut out to the pencil line. Do not cut the bottom of the tree or border at 'Y'. Open out to find two trees (c).

3. a.b.
**   c.d.** Try the same tree again, using a little larger piece of paper. Fold in half (a), and half again length ways (b). Now fold bottom to top. Draw this outline and cut out (c). When opened, does yours look like this? (d).

4. a.b.
**   c.** Try another design, following the folding and cutting as in **1**, **2**, and **3** (above). A single fold (a), a single fold and then bottom to top (b), and finally two folds and bottom to top (c).

5. a.b. It is not always easy to draw and then cut out a round flower head, but try this method. Draw the half square from the fold, add the corner lines to guide you like this (a). Then you can make small snips out when cutting away the unwanted paper (b).

Remember, to give a neater edge, pierce the unwanted paper as shown at 'X' in the folded papers, and cut out to the drawn line. Stick the cutouts very carefully to the coloured cartridge paper and press them down well, covering them first with blotting paper.

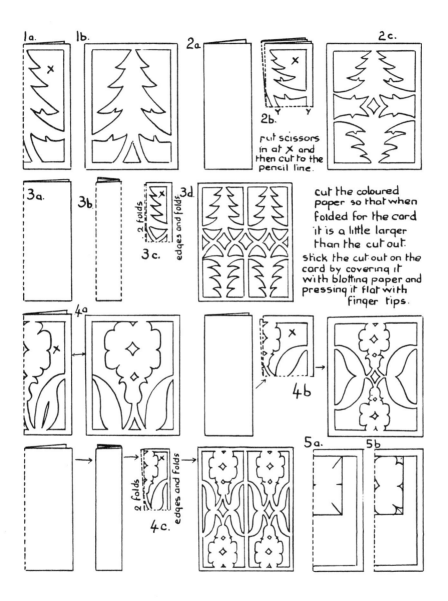

1a. 1b.

2a.

2c.

2b.

cut scissors in at X and then cut to the pencil line.

3a. 3b.

2 folds

3c.

edges and folds

3d.

cut the coloured paper so that when folded for the card it is a little larger than the cut out.

stick the cut out on the card by covering it with blotting paper and pressing it flat with finger tips.

4a.

X

4b.

2 folds

edges and folds

4c.

5a. 5b.

69

CUT PAPER CARDS

Materials: a. Thin black or coloured paper, gummed or plain
               b. White gummed paper
               c. White or coloured cartridge paper
               d. Paste, if not using gummed paper
               e. Scrap paper to practise on   f. Scissors
               g. Pencil   h. White crayon
               i. Pinking shears   j. Punch for holes

Paper cutting is a very old skill. Any gift card with a cut paper design is attractive. These cards can be cut from black paper to be pasted on to white or coloured card, or cut in white to be pasted on to black paper. Coloured cut outs can be pasted on to either.

1. a.b. This one is cut from white paper which is folded in half (a).
    c. A simple half design is lightly drawn on it from the folded edge (b). When cutting out, any part which is actually on the fold is left uncut. When opened out the result is as (c), and pasted on to coloured card.

2. a.b. This example was cut from black paper and mounted on to white card. When using black paper, a white crayon is used to draw the design (a).

3. a.b. This is a little more difficult as it has a border to it, which is cut out at the same time. Draw the design on the folded paper. Cut away the pieces between the design first, by pushing the point of the scissors through the folded paper at 'X' and 'X' (a) and then cut out to the pencilled line of the design and border. To make an interesting variation of this, paste it on to a piece of black paper of the same size. Then mount it on to coloured card (b).

4. a.b. Long borders are fun to do. They go right across the top and
    c. bottom of the card, leaving the centre free for the greeting. Cut a strip of paper the length of the card and fold it in half (a) and in half again (b). The design was drawn and cut out (this one was for a child) and pasted across the card.

5. a.b. These borders were folded as in 4(a) and (b) (above), then folded smaller once again and cut out. Remember that the more the paper is folded, the harder it is to cut neatly, so a thinner paper is required here.

A paper punch for making small circles is a great help in making patterns like those on the butterfly in 1 (above), and pinking shears for cutting the edge in 5(b).

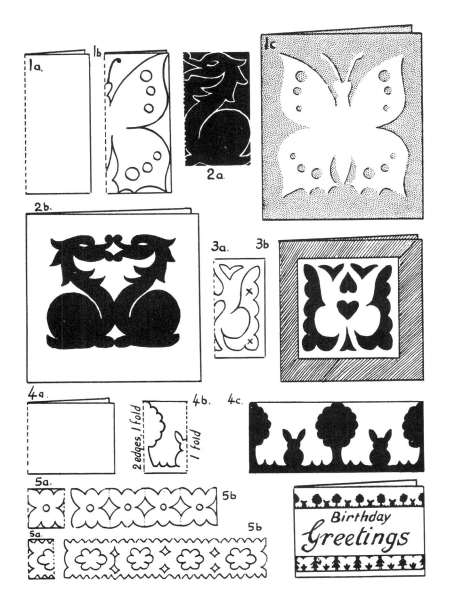

1a. 1b 1c

2a.

2b.

3a. 3b

4a. 4b. 4c.

2 edges, 1 fold 1 fold

5a. 5b

5a. 5b

Birthday
Greetings

EASTER EGG CHICKEN

Materials: a. Three plain white postcards *or* b. Thin white card
                   c. Colours   d. Scissors
                   e. Pencil and ruler   f. Glue

1. Cut three pieces of card the same size 14cm x 5cm (5.5" x 2") or, if using postcards, cut a 4cm (1.75") strip from one side of each. Also cut two strips of card 14cm x 1cm (5.5" x .5"). Find the centre of each side on one of the cards and draw a light line across.

2. a.b. From the centre line downwards draw an egg-cup, with the body touching both sides. Do not make the stem part too narrow. It should be at least 2cm (.75"). On the line across the top of the egg-cup draw the ragged edge of a cracked egg. Keep it simple, not too ragged (a). Cut out round the egg-shell and cup (b).

3. The second card has a line drawn across it 2.5cm (1") from the bottom. Lay the bottom line of your cut-out egg-cup on this line. Draw very carefully round it and remove.

4. a.b. From the cracked egg edge of this second card, draw half an egg shape. Note that it must not touch the sides of the card (a). Under the cracked egg-shell line draw a chicken's body like this (b). Keep its body well inside the outline of the egg-cup. It must not touch it. In the centre of the card below the chicken, rule two lines 1cm (.5") apart down to the edge of the card.

5. Cut out the egg-shell, the chicken and the strip at the bottom all in one. Cut a long strip of card 1cm (.5") wide. Glue it over the bottom strip, and up into the body a little, to strengthen it. Colour the chicken and shell.

6. a.b. Lay the egg-cup you cut out in 1 (above) on the third card and draw round it. Cut this out. Cut off the broken shell leaving the egg-cup straight at the top (a). Put a little glue just round the sides only of the egg-cup (see shading (a)) very carefully, stick the first egg-cup cut-out over the top of it (b).

7. When firmly stuck together, gently push the long strip of card down inside, between the two halves of the egg-cup. Pull gently through the unstuck gap left at the bottom, until the broken edges of the shell meet.

8. Colour the egg-cup. The greetings can be written on the front or back of the cup. Push the strip up gently and there is your chicken. The long strip could be made stronger by sticking two strips together.

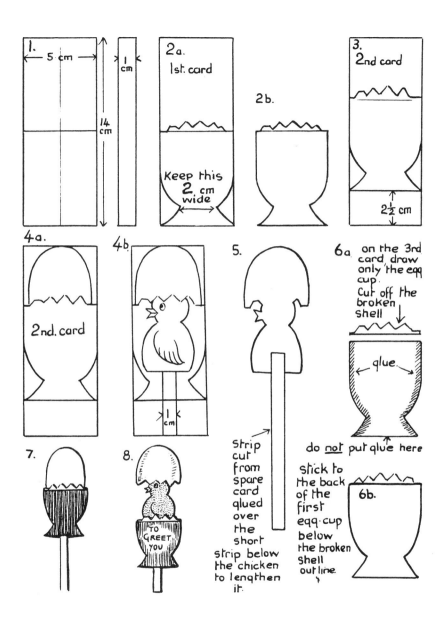

1. ← 5 cm → | 1 cm | 14 cm

2a. 1st. card

2b.

Keep this 2 cm wide

3. 2nd card

2½ cm

4a. 2nd. card

4b. 1 cm

5. Strip cut from spare card glued over the short strip below the chicken to lengthen it.

6a. on the 3rd card, draw only the egg cup.
Cut off the broken shell
glue
do **not** put glue here
Stick to the back of the first egg cup below the broken shell outline.

6b.

7.

8. TO GREET YOU

73

HALLOWE'EN INVITATION

Materials: a. Two plain postcards
              b. Small brass two-pronged paper-clip
              c. Cup
              d. Scissors   e. Pencil and ruler
              f. Small pin   g. Glue

1. Measure each edge of the postcards with the ruler to find the centre and draw a line across in each direction. Where the lines cross in the centre, prick a hole with the pin. Do this in both cards.

2. Rule another line 7mm (.25") above the centre line on each card.

3. Lay one card aside for the moment. Cut the other card right across on the upper line. This will be for the church tower.

4. Measure off nine equal spaces across the top of the card, and draw in the battlements like this. Cut off a narrow strip either side of the tower. Draw in the clock face and add the stonework. The hands should be drawn in to show the time the party is to start.

5. Using the cup or other round object draw a large circle on the second card. This must not be wider than the tower, so measure that first. The circle represents the moon, and should touch the top edge of the card. Inside the moon circle draw a witch holding a paper on which the wording of the invitation is to be written. Cut round the moon, and colour.

6. Turn the card round and draw a fleecy cloud on the other half. Add stars and a small bat or two. Here again the cloud must not be wider than the tower or the moon. Cut out your card. It should look like this.

7. Push just the point of the scissors gently into the pin holes to make them a little larger. Then push the two prongs of the paper-clip through the tower and then through the second card, and bend the prongs back. Turn the witch round so that the tower hides her.

8. To read your invitation your guest must twist the cloud round to allow the witch to appear with tidings. For a variation an owl can be drawn on the moon shape.

1.

2.
↓7mm
×

3.

4.
mark off 9 equal
spaces across here

5.
×width of the tower×

6.

7.

8.
INVITATION
TO A
HALLOWEEN
PARTY ON

YOU ARE INVITED
TO A
HALLOWEEN PARTY

CHRISTMAS ROBIN ON A STUMP

Materials:
    a. Two plain postcards
    b. White gummed paper
    c. Cotton wool
    d. Small brass two-pronged paper-clip
    e. Scissors
    f. Pencil and ruler
    g. Colours
    h. Small pin

1. This is similar to the witch Hallowe'en invitation card. Find the centre of each side of the two cards and draw light pencil lines across. Make a small hole in the centre where the lines cross.

2. a.b. Draw a post or tree stump on one of the cards, with a layer of snow on it, which rises above the pin-hole (a). Now cut it out (b).

3. Put the cut-out tree stump on top of the second card. Draw lightly round its outline, and remove it. Above the snowline on this second card draw a robin, with its legs and tail in the snow like this. It must not be wider than the width of the stump. Below the snowline, and within the outline of the stump, draw a cloud of falling snowflakes.

4. Cut the robin and cloud out as here. Colour them. With the point of the scissors make the pinhole in each card slightly larger.

5. Turn the robin upside down, and with the cloud at the top place the cut-out tree stump over the top. Make sure the robin's head does not show under the bottom of the stump. Then gently push the paper-clip through the hole in the stump card first, then the robin's card and bend the prongs back.

6. Turn the cloud round and down to make the robin appear.

7. You may like to stick a little cotton wool over the paper clip to represent snow.

8. For your greetings, cut a piece of white paper and stick on to the tree stump to write them on, or simply write them on the back.

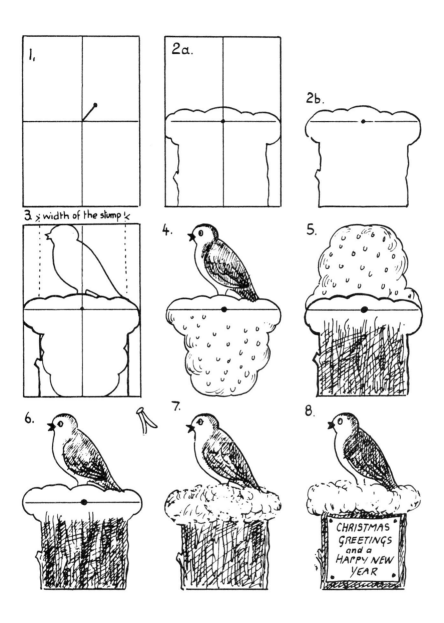

1.

2a.

2b.

3. ⟩⟨ width of the stump ⟩⟨

4.

5.

6.

7.

8.

CHRISTMAS
GREETINGS
and a
HAPPY NEW
YEAR

'DONKEY RIDING' BIRTHDAY CARD

Materials: a. Two plain postcards or thin white card
                b. Tracing paper
                c. Colours
                d. Scissors
                e. Pencil
                f. Paste

If you are not much good at drawing, you can make tracings of this boy and donkey to use for your card.

1. Fold one of the cards in half and draw on it the outline of the donkey's body. The back of the donkey must be on the fold. Make the front end of the donkey come to the edge on the left, and the tail to the edge of the right.

2. Open the card and cut out round the drawn line, but not between the legs.

3. a.b. Close the card. Pencil round the outline you cut out on to the half card underneath. Now cut that half shape out but do not cut the fold (a). Cut a small slit along the fold in the centre (b). Draw in the legs and ground.

4. On the second card draw the child and the donkey's head with a long neck. Cut out both of them. Now colour them. Make a small slit at 'X'.

5. Stick the long neck of the donkey inside the front half of the body in a straight line at the top by the fold.

6. Slide the left leg of the rider inside the slit in the donkey's back. Put paste on the leg inside the body to stop the rider falling off.

7. Pull the donkey's legs apart a little to make him stand up. Write your greetings on the uncut card between the legs, or inside the card.

You may well find a similar donkey or other animal in a magazine that you could use. Cut it out and paste on to a folded card. Finish it off as above.

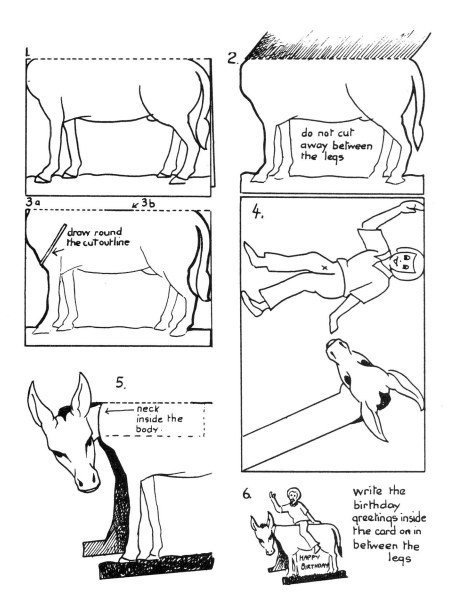

1.

2. do not cut away between the legs

3a. 3b.
draw round the cut outline

4.

5. neck inside the body

6. HAPPY BIRTHDAY

write the birthday greetings inside the card on in between the legs

CAT HALLOWE'EN INVITATION

Materials: a. Thin white card
             b. Black paint or ink
             c. Colour, brick-red
             d. Sellotape
             e. Pencil
             f. Scissors
             g. Black cotton
             h. Ruler
             i. Paste

1. a.b. For this you need a strip of card 32cm x 8cm (12.75" x 3.25"). Fold in half (a). On the top part of the card, measure 9cm (3.5") up from the bottom and draw a line across (b).

2. Draw a cat on this line. Make sure that its back and tail touch the fold at the top.

3. a.b. The cat is now cut out, both sides together, but DO NOT cut the back and tail where they touch the fold (a). If you find cutting both sides together too difficult, then cut out the top card on its own. Close the card, draw round the cut out, on to the card beneath and then cut that one out. Be careful when cutting the top (b). Measure 3cm (1.25") up from the bottom of the card back and front, and bend it under inside the card. This will make a stand for the card. Scoring the line first will make it easier to bend.

4. Colour the cat black, with a white eye, and colour the wall brick-red, leaving strips of white card between the bricks. Stick four or five short lengths of black cotton behind the cat for whiskers, using sellotape. Write the invitation on the wall in black.

By painting the cat grey, ginger or tabby, this could be used for a child's party.

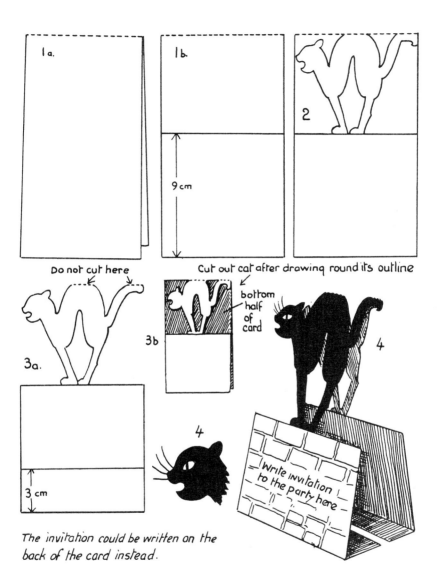

1a.

1b.

9 cm

2

Do not cut here

Cut out cat after drawing round its outline

bottom half of card

3a.

3b

3 cm

4

4

Write invitation to the party here

The invitation could be written on the back of the card instead.

WITCH INVITATION CARD

Materials: a. White cartridge paper
                 b. Black indian ink or black paint
                 c. Paint brush
                 d. Pencil
                 e. Scissors
                 f. Tracing paper
                 g. Newspaper

1. a.b. Trace off this witch (a), or draw your own. Turn the tracing over and draw over the pencil line again (b).

2. Fold a piece of paper for the card and lay the tracing on it. Make sure that the cloak, broom and skirt come right on to the fold on the left. Go over the tracing again, so that it comes through on to the card beneath. Cut round this outline, but DO NOT cut the fold where the cloak, broom and skirt touch it.

3. Open the cut-out and lay it flat on a sheet of newspaper. Very carefully, paint all over it with the paint or ink. It is difficult to prevent the black from smudging on the underside of the cut-out, so when the first side is dry, turn it over and black that side too. The invitation can be written on a piece of white or coloured paper and pasted inside.

Note: It is possible to obtain black poster paper which is white inside. This is ideal for the witch. Simply fold the paper white side out, transfer your tracing of the witch on to it as in 2 (above). Cut it out neatly, and refold with the black side out. No need to use black ink, except perhaps for the invitation inside.

1a.

1b. tracing

2.

3. newspaper

4.

STANDING CHICKEN FOR EASTER

Materials: a. Small piece of white paper
             b. Yellow paper or thin card
             c. Tracing paper
             d. Two round lids of different sizes
             e. Felt pen
             f. Scissors
             g. Pencil
             h. Paste

If you have not got a compass to make the circles here, lids of two different sizes can be used. They should be about 4cm (1.5") for the head and about 6cm (2.5") for the body.

1. Put the lids on the yellow paper and draw round them.

2. Add the tail and legs to the larger circle and cut out. The head is cut out without addition.

3. Stick the head behind the body circle, a little near the top, on the opposite side to the tail, and make a straight cut up the legs to the body.

4. Cut a small piece of yellow, or better still, orange paper to make the beak. Cut a small circle in white for the eye, draw in the black pupil and stick both on. See 7 (below).

5. Draw the wing on yellow paper and cut it out. Lay the wing in place on the body and very lightly draw round it. Write your Easter greetings inside the pencil line, then rub out the lines. See **3** (above).

6. a.b. Lay the bottom of the chicken body and legs on yellow paper and draw round the legs (a). Remove the chicken and add the extra bit to the top of your drawing, coming to a point and cut out. Make a straight cut down from the point to the centre (b).

7. a.b. Stick the wing to the body, but paste only where marked 'XX', so that the wing can be lifted to show your message (a). Slide the extra bit you cut for the legs into the slit of the chicken's legs until the two bottoms are level and stand it up (b).

1.

4 cm
Head

Two lids to draw round

Body 6 cm

2.

yellow paper

3.

A
HAPPY EASTER
TO YOU
from ....

4

beak

eye

cut

5.

6a.

6b

cut

7a

Stick only the wing at X to the body

7b.

8.

A
HAPPY
EASTER

TWO SNOWMEN CARDS

Materials: a. Blue cartridge paper
                  b. White embossed wallpaper or plain white paper
                  c. Green, black and red gummed paper
                  d. Round lids of three different sizes
                  e. Scissors   f. Paste
                  g. Pencil   h. Cotton wool

First Snowman:

Cut and fold the blue paper, large enough to take the three lids comfortably on it.

Using the lids (or a compass) draw and cut out three circles from the white or embossed paper. Cut a strip to go across the bottom of the card for snow.

Paste the largest circle on the card first, near the base of the card. Paste the middle-sized circle on, overlapping the large one a little, then the small one, again overlapping a little.

Cut a black hat from the gummed paper for his head, two red hands, red nose, black buttons and eyes, and a part circle of red or green for the scarf. Stick all in place. The snow strip goes across the bottom and just over the large circle a little.

Second Snowman:

This fellow is drawn, a circle for the head, and a longish oval for the body, and two small ovals for the arms. Cover the inside of all the circles and ovals with paste and stick on small tufts of cotton wool for snow. Paste some along the bottom too.

Cut out a hat of some kind. This one wears a green tammy. Cut a scarf. This one is red. Give him red hands, nose and mouth, and black buttons and eyes as above for the first snowman. These must all be stuck firmly to the cotton wool, so put a little paste on the gummed paper to make it stick more strongly.

To make it easier to cut two hands the same, fold a long strip of paper in half, so that it is a square. Draw a hand on this and cut both sides out together.

The greetings can be written inside, or cut from old cards and stuck in.

3 circles for body in White

red hands

red nose

scarf red or green

green tammy

blue card

pencil outline

blue card

'STAND-OUT' CARDS

Materials: a. Old greeting cards
            b. Calendar of views, travel magazines
            c. Coloured cartridge paper   d. Thin card
            e. Scissors   f. Paste
            g. Ruler   h. Pencil

Look through a magazine or calendar for an attractive picture. It can be of the countryside, hills, town, garden or seashore, etc.

1. a.b The paper for the card (a) must be twice the size of the picture,
c. so when it is folded the picture just fits it. The paper is folded in half (b), in half again (c), and opened out.

2. The selected picture is pasted flat on to the folded card, and allowed to dry thoroughly. It can then be folded down the centre again.

3. a.b. Look through the magazine or old cards for a suitable figure to add to your picture. It should not be too large – smaller than the width of the right-hand side of your card (a). In the drawing here the cut-out swan did not touch either the centre fold or edge of the card (b). If the figure is on thin paper, it should be pasted first on to card and cut out when dry.

4. Cut a strip of card 7.5cm (3") long and about 1cm (.5") wide. Measure and divide into three equal parts of 2.5cm (1"), and bend it like this.

5. Paste the part marked 'X' to the back of your figure, in the centre and at the bottom of it.

6. a.b. Open the card full out. From the bottom edge of the right-hand
c. side of the card, and in the centre of it, measure up 2.5cm (1") and make a pencil mark slightly longer than the width of the thin strip. With the point of the scissors, very carefully cut along that mark to make a slit (a). Put paste on the back of the card above the slit, push the end of the strip marked 'Z' through it and bend up to stick to the back of the picture (b). Push the cut-out figure gently up on the folds in the strip and gently close the card (c). When opened the cut-out figure will stand forward. Write the greetings on the front.

7.&8. It can be quite as effective if the picture and figure are cut for the right-hand half of the card only. Then the greetings verse or message can be written or pasted on the left-hand side.

1b.

1c.

2

3b

3a.

$7\frac{1}{2}$ cm

4.

z

x

5.

back

z

x

6a.

cut

6b

back of the picture cut

6c.

6c.

HAPPY FATHERS DAY

7.

8.

NIGHT SCENES

Materials: a. Black cartridge paper
                b. White cartridge paper
                c. Old greeting cards, magazines, etc.
                d. Newspaper to work on
                e. Scissors
                f. Paste and brush
                g. Narrow ribbon or cord

The card here is for Christmas, but similar cards can be made for any occasion. It is in the form of a collage, which means making a picture out of parts of other pictures stuck on to a base. Pictures from old cards, magazines, old calendars and so on can be used to great effect.

1. Cut out small houses, figures, trees, a church, a stable, sheep, shepherds, wise men, anything that has a Christmassy connection.

2. a.b. Decide upon the size of the card you want, and cut it out of black paper. Fold it in half, then open it out flat on newspaper in front on you. You can make the picture on the right-hand side of the crease, which will form the front of the card when folded (a) or right across the card which will then be folded so that the scene is on the inside of the card (b). Whichever you decide on, arrange cut-outs on the black background, moving them around until you achieve the effect that pleases you most. When satisfied, paste them in one by one. In the night sky, stick on bought stars, or paint your own in yellow or white.

2. a. For this, cut the white paper the same size as the card and slip it inside, fastening them together with narrow ribbon or cord. Your greetings go inside.

2. b. Use the white paper as the cover in this case, writing your message on the outside. Put a little paste on the back of the right-hand side of the black paper and stick it inside the white.

Two further designs to show what different scenes can look like.

2a.

2b.

MOSAIC WALL HANGING

Materials: a. Sheet of brown wrapping paper or light coloured paper
b. Coloured magazines and other papers
c. Roll of gummed paper strip (brown)
d. Coloured gummed paper   e. Drawing pins
f. Paints   g. Blotting paper
h. Scissors   i. Paste and brush
j. Pencil   k. Cocktail stick
l. Two dowel rods   m. String

Here is something quite different – a mosaic greetings wall hanging. It is made from small pieces of coloured paper pasted piece by piece on a background to form a picture. There is great scope for originality here.

1. Cut strips of paper about 1cm to 1.5cm (approximately .5") wide of any length. These strips are cut into small shapes like this: squares, triangles, diamonds or any odd shape, as shown here. Circles are not very suitable for this, but cutting the corners off a square makes a better fit.

2. The background of light coloured or brown wrapping paper is better if strengthened with brown gummed paper bought in a roll. It will also prevent the edges from curling up.

3. Draw the outline of the subject that you have in mind on the front of the paper. It can be a plant, figure, animal, bird, abstract pattern or any other object, but keep it bold and simple. Work round the outline of the design first, by putting paste on the tiny pieces of paper of the desired colour, and sticking them down, leaving a space between each piece. Do this round the outline of each part of the design. The cocktail stick, or something similar, will be of help to push each piece into the exact place it should be. Press down firmly with the blotting paper, which will absorb any surplus paste which may ooze out from under the shapes. If using gummed paper, dampen each piece and place into position in the same way, piece by piece.

4. When you have completed the outline, begin filling in the rest of the figure, remembering to leave a small gap between each piece. Use the odd shapes to fill in awkward corners. The whole of the background can be filled in, or simply painted and left plain. Faces are difficult to do, so cut one from a magazine, or paint one in. Then stick mosaic pieces all round it. When quite finished, lay the hanging between clean paper under a weight to dry really flat. To hang, pin the picture to the dowels at the top and bottom, and tie on a length of string.

Mosaic can be used for cards, but needs very small pieces so try the wall hanging first to get your hand in.

1.

1 cm. or 1½ cm

2. back of the wall hanging

brown gummed paper to strengthen edges

3. HAPPY DAY MUM

4. HAPPY DAY MUM

HAPPY BIRTHDAY

WELCOME HOME

WELCOME BABY

ENLARGING OR REDUCING BY SQUARING-OFF METHOD

Materials: a. Drawing paper   b. Tracing paper
                  c. Paper-clips   d. Ruler
                  e. Pencil   f. Rubber

You may find you want a larger or smaller copy of some item in this or some other book to use for your cards. Here is a method to help you to get over this problem. It is possible to enlarge or reduce a picture by using a grid like this.

1. Make a grid like this on tracing paper to cover the picture you wish to enlarge. The grid must cover the picture completely top to bottom and side to side. Make all the lines up and down across at equal distances apart. The grid is drawn on tracing paper to save damage to the picture, but if the picture does not matter the grid can be drawn straight on to it.

2. Number all the lines across and up and down.

3. On your card, measure the size you want your drawing to be enlarged or reduced to. Divide this up into the exact number of squares as on the grid on the tracing paper or picture, and number them in the same way.

4. Very carefully secure the tracing paper over the picture with paper-clips.

5. Now look closely at the outline of the picture and start copying it square by square on to the squares on your drawing paper, making sure that the square on the drawing corresponds with the square on the picture according to the numbers on the squares. Take your time over it. You will find it gets easier as you become more accustomed to it.

6. To make a small drawing of the picture the squares on the drawing paper are made smaller, but the same principle is involved, copying square by square according to the numbers on the picture and the drawing paper.

Here the grid in 3 and 5 is twice the size of the grid in 1, 2, and 4.

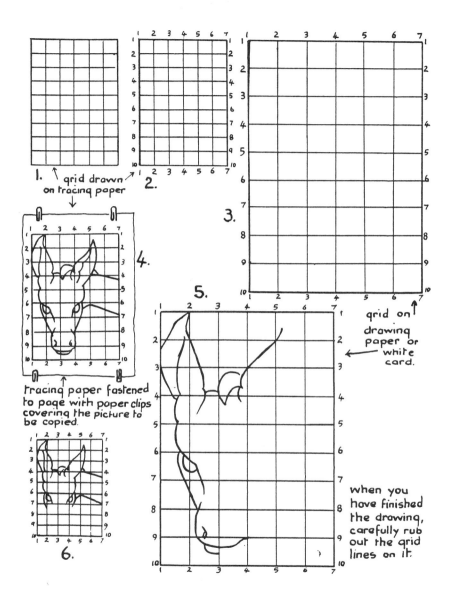

1. ↑ grid drawn → on tracing paper

2.

3.

4.

5.

6.

grid on drawing paper or white card.

tracing paper fastened to page with paper clips covering the picture to be copied.

when you have finished the drawing, carefully rub out the grid lines on it.

LIST OF SEASONS,
SPECIAL OCCASIONS AND INVITATIONS

The following is a list of some of the occasions on which you may wish to send a card of greetings or an invitation to some gathering. You may think of others.

Greetings:

Birthday
Christening
Christmas
Congratulations
Easter
Father's Day
Get Well
Good Voyage
Mother's Day
New Baby
New Home
New Year
Retirement
St. Valentine's Day
Thank You
Wedding Anniversary
Wedding Day
Welcome Home

Invitations:

Birthday Party
Christening
Christmas Party
Hallowe'en Party
New Year Party
Wedding

Greetings for all occasions:

Wall Hanging

A LIST OF WEDDING ANNIVERSARIES

1st	Paper		14th	Ivory
2nd	Cotton		15th	Crystal
3rd	Leather		20th	China
4th	Silk (Flowers, Fruit)		25th	Silver
5th	Wood		30th	Pearl
6th	Iron		35th	Coral
7th	Copper		40th	Ruby
8th	Bronze		45th	Sapphire
9th	Pottery		50th	Gold
10th	Tin		55th	Emerald
11th	Steel		60th	Diamond
12th	Linen		65th	Platinum
13th	Lace			